Brown

Do You Remember the '60s?

- The college athlete who went from gridiron greatness to the Court Supreme?
- Smell-o-vision?
- Dick Nixon declaring that he "can't stand Pat?"
- A hirsute counter-tenor trampling on tulips?
- "Marvelous Marv's" bogus base-running blunder?

Other Avon Books by
Bill Adler

DO YOU REMEMBER THE '50s?
500 GREAT FACTS ABOUT AMERICA
100 WAYS TO LOVE AMERICA

DO YOU REMEMBER THE '60s?

Bill Adler

AVON BOOKS NEW YORK

DO YOU REMEMBER THE '60's? is an original publication of Avon Books. This work has never before appeared in book form.

AVON BOOKS
A division of
The Hearst Corporation
1350 Avenue of the Americas
New York, New York 10019

Cover design by FPG International
Published by arrangement with the author
Library of Congress Catalog Card Number: 92-90329
ISBN: 0-380-76733-3

First Avon Books Printing: December 1992

Printed in the U.S.A.

RA 10 9 8 7 6 5 4 3 2 1

1960

"If Ever I Would Leave You." Princess Margaret of Great Britain marries photographer Anthony-Armstrong Jones, Caryl Chessman is finally executed in the gas chamber at San Quentin after eight reprieves and the penning of a best-selling book, and Israeli agents succeed in capturing Nazi death camp chief Adolf Eichmann in Argentina. The American Heart Association fingers heavy smoking as a cause of heart attacks among middle-aged men.

The world of the arts is staggered by the deaths of so many major figures, including silent film comedy master Mack Sennett, writers Richard Wright, Boris Pasternak, and *Grand Hotel* novelist Vicki Baum, composer Oscar Hammerstein II, conductor Dimitri Mitropoulos, and incomparable tenor Jussi Bjoerling. The year also brings the death of Emily Post, sparing her the travails of a very uncivil decade.

Floyd Patterson takes the heavyweight boxing crown back from Ingemar Johansson, and the New York Yankees, despite two shutouts thrown by Whitey Ford, lose a wild seven-game Series to the Pittsburgh Pirates when Bill Maseroski breaks a ninth-inning 9–9 tie with a booming home run.

The 1960s were marked by vast gatherings of Americans in open spaces, brought together in some instances for reasons of joy and entertainment, but too often in protest or in sorrow. Connect the events in the left-hand column below with the number of attendees in the right-hand column.

1. Gathered in Washington, D.C., for the "Jobs and Freedom March" and heard Martin Luther King deliver his "I have a dream" speech in 1963.	a. 700,000
2. Waited in line for hours and managed to get into the Capitol Rotunda to pass the bier of John F. Kennedy in 1963.	b. 50,000
3. Assembled at the Lincoln Memorial in protest of the war in Vietnam in 1967.	c. 185,000
4. Marched down Fifth Avenue in New York City to support war in Vietnam, 1967.	d. 400,000
5. Gathered along the rail route from New York to Washington to watch Robert F. Kennedy's funeral train pass by, in 1968.	e. 250,000
6. Swarmed onto six-hundred-acre farm near Woodstock, New York, to hear the greatest rock concert in history, in 1969.	f. 2,000,000

1, e; 2, c; 3, b; 4, a; 5, f; 6, d

What Nobel Prize–winning author, whose first novel was a favorite on college campuses, died in an automobile accident at the age of forty-seven in 1960?

Albert Camus, author of *The Stranger*.

What does "light amplification by stimulated emission of radiation" describe?

The laser, first devised in 1960.

What was *Tiros I*, and how did it help improve one segment of the evening news?

It was the first weather satellite, put up by the United States to monitor worldwide cloud patterns, thus making possible better long-range forecasting.

Name the great American opera singer who dropped dead of a heart attack while performing onstage at the Metropolitan Opera.

Leonard Warren

In the late fifties, a very pretty young actress made her film debut in two Rogers and Hammerstein musicals. Obviously, she could sing like a lark. But in 1960 she won an Academy Award for a nonsinging role. Name the actress and the film.

Shirley Jones, who played a prostitute in *Elmer Gantry*.

This 1960 Oscar-winning song instructed us not to do something on a certain day of the week. Name the song. And what were we not supposed to do on that day?

"Never on Sunday," music and lyrics by Manos Hadjidakis. In a lighthearted way, we were advised not to make love on the Sabbath.

This Hollywood sex goddess and her French costar took the title of their new movie a bit too seriously. Name them and the film.

Marilyn Monroe and Yves Montand. They managed to have an affair that landed them on the cover of *Life* magazine. The name of the film was *Let's Make Love*.

In 1960 a Scottish-born actress received her sixth Oscar nomination as Best Actress—and lost again. Name the actress and the movie.

Deborah Kerr received her sixth nomination for *The Sundowners*. She had previously been nominated for *Edward My Son* (1949), *From Here to Eternity* (1953), *The King and I* (1956), *Heaven Knows Mr. Allison* (1957), and *Separate Tables* (1958). The Oscars for those years went to, in order, Olivia De Havilland for *The Heiress*, Audrey Hepburn for *Roman Holiday*, Ingrid Bergman for *Anastasia*, Joanne Woodward for *Three Faces of Eve*, Susan Hayward for *I Want to Live*, and in 1960 Elizabeth Taylor for *Butterfield 8*. To this day she holds the record for most nominations for Best Actress without a win and, to the Academy's shame, has not even been given an honorary Oscar.

Throughout the thirties, forties, and fifties, this singer was called "Miss Perfect Pitch." But in 1960 she won Best Comedy Album of the Year by singing flat and sharp. Name her and the album.

Jo Stafford. She and her husband/pianist Paul Weston won for their screamingly funny album, *Jonathan and Darlene Edwards in Paris*.

What was John F. Kennedy's campaign song in 1960?

The song was adapted from Sammy Cahn and Jimmy Van Heusens's "High Hopes," written for the motion picture *A Hole in the Head*.

John Wayne acted in and produced the 1960 film *The Alamo*. It was nominated for six Oscars, including Best Picture. It garnered one for Best Sound. Many Texans got a big laugh over this film. Why?

Because Mr. Wayne insisted that the Alamo look like a

huge, aging hotel when it is actually a small building. "Motel" would be more descriptive.

In an interview, Ethel Merman said that her favorite Broadway singing costar was ———?

a. Bruce Yarnell *(Annie Get Your Gun)*
b. Bert Lahr *(Du Barry Was a Lady)*
c. Jack Klugman *(Gypsy)*

The answer is c. Miss Merman's praise for Mr. Klugman amused many people, because he couldn't sing his way out of a paper bag. Thus, no vocal competition.

On a quieter note, in 1960 these young men recorded four albums that sold over a million copies each, somewhat of a record to this day. What did they call themselves?

The Kingston Trio. Remember "Scotch and Soda" and "The Green Leaves of Summer"?

What comedian won the 1960 Grammy Award for Album of the Year, much to the dismay of many?

Bob Newhart for *Button Down Mind*. The dismay was felt by musicians, who thought that music was what the Grammys were about.

In 1960 Michael Todd, Jr., came up with a new idea that he was sure would thrill American moviegoers. What was it?

Smell-O-Vision. It was a total flop. Movie patrons complained that they just could not hold their breath for two hours. The few who could complained that they could not see the movie because so many were running to the theater rest rooms for a breath of fresh air.

This actress said of her latest film, "I still say it stinks." However, she won the 1960 Academy Award for Best Actress. Name her and the film.

Elizabeth Taylor for *Butterfield 8.*

In 1960 the Ford Motor Company introduced a new car that became the butt of many jokes. For example: A man comes into the office sobbing uncontrollably. His coworkers ask, "What's the matter, Hank? Is it Marge? Is it the kids?" *"No,"* he sobbed. Why was that man crying?

That man had bought an Edsel.

Another car, introduced by General Motors in the early sixties with much fanfare, was a major flop. One national magazine wrote, "The ——— is the perfect economy car. It never starts." Fill in the blank.

The Corvair, which has since become one of the most sought-after models by car collectors. *If* you have the cash on hand.

Before the Edsel and the Corvair were even on the drawing board, two other dogs were reigning supreme on weekly nighttime television. Name them.

Lassie and Rin Tin Tin. Both dogs probably outlived the above-mentioned cars.

The sixties ushered in a huge crop of memorable songs. Some of them will never be forgotten. For instance, "Itsy Bitsy, Teenie Weenie, Yellow Polka-Dot Bikini." Who wrote the music and lyrics to this mind-broadening masterpiece?

Paul J. Vance and Lee Pockriss, who went on to the heights of oblivion.

After the huge success of the "Beetle," Volkswagon manufactured a sports car that was mostly ignored by Americans. What was it called?

The Dual Ghia.

This 1960 thriller's promotion was "No one will be admitted after the picture has started." It was also the first movie to photograph the flushing of a toilet. Name it.

Alfred Hitchcock's *Psycho*

One of Lyndon B. Johnson's favorite crude jokes had to do with what an intellectual does or does not do in the shower. What was his punch line?

"An intellectual steps out of the shower to take a leak."

This television couple and their two sons reminded us every week what an American family should look and be like. Name the show.

"The Adventures of Ozzie and Harriet," which ran from 1952 to 1966. The most adventurous thing that ever happened on this show was whose turn it was to mow the lawn. The subject of toilets was never brought up.

Two-time Academy Award winner Sally Field first became famous in two 1960s television series. Can you name them?

"Gidget" and "The Flying Nun."

In 1960, while being interviewed by the press on national television, the very pregnant Jackie Kennedy was asked if the baby would be born by Inauguration Day. What was her reply?

She asked when Inauguration Day was.

In the early sixties, McDonald's was already a thriving fast-food chain. How much did a burger cost?

A whopping fifteen cents

The 1960 census revealed that for the first time, a major American city had a population that was more than 50 percent black. Which city scored this first?

Washington, D.C.

A very important man called a man soon to be equally important a "whippersnapper" in 1960. Name both men.

President Eisenhower thought John F. Kennedy was far too young and inexperienced to be president.

What was the special significance of Kennedy's primary win over Hubert Humphrey in West Virginia?

The Catholic population of the state was very small, and Kennedy's win showed that he had defused worries about his being a Catholic.

Why did Richard Nixon have to spend almost two weeks in the hospital at the start of the 1960 fall campaign against John F. Kennedy?

He bumped his knee on the door of his limousine, and the wound became infected.

What did "jumpers" have to do with the presidential campaign, and who were they?

They were young women who jumped up and down as Kennedy's motorcades passed them during the campaign.

Although most were too young to vote, they suggested the growing undercurrent of enthusiasm for the charismatic young candidate.

This woman had had such a severe case of polio as a child that she did not start walking, with the aid of a leg brace, until she was eight years old. But at the 1960 Summer Olympics in Rome, she won three Gold medals in Track and Field. Name her.

Wilma Rudolph. Stricken as a child with double pneumonia, scarlet fever, and finally polio, this seventeenth child in a family of nineteen children had been taken by her mother on a ninety-mile trip each week to a free clinic. At home her mother massaged Wilma's legs for hours every day. By the time she was in her early teens, Wilma Rudolph began to show signs of phenomenal ability. At Rome she set an Olympic record for the Hundred-Meter Sprint, a world record in the Two-Hundred-Meter Dash, and anchored the American Four-Hundred-Meter Women's Relay Team, which also set a new world record.

What heavyweight boxing champion regained his crown at the Polo Grounds in 1960? And whom did he defeat?

Twenty-five-year-old Floyd Patterson, who took the heavyweight title back from Ingemar Johansson.

No one was much surprised when this athlete won the Olympic Gold Medal for the decathlon at the 1960 games. He had set a world record in the event two years earlier when he was the president of the UCLA student body. Name him.

Rafer Johnson was the very model of the student athlete and Olympian. Twenty-six years later, he was given the honor of lighting the Olympic torch at the opening of the Los Angeles games.

In 1960 this famed left fielder hit a home run in his last at-bat before retirement, but refused to tip his hat to the wildly cheering home crowd. Name him.

Ted Williams, who had always had a prickly relationship with Boston Red Sox fans.

At the 1960 Summer Olympics, the U.S. women's swimming team won the first of four successive Gold Medals, and the men's team the first of five in the same respective event. What was it?

The Women's and Men's Four-Hundred-Meter Medley Relay.

In the first year of play for the new American Football League, the Los Angeles Raiders quarterback led the league in passing. Name this future congressman, presidential candidate, and cabinet member.

Jack Kemp racked up 3,018 yards and twenty touchdown passes.

How did President Eisenhower get himself into trouble talking about weather planes that weren't?

On May 1, 1960, sixteen days before a summit with Khrushchev, de Gaulle, and Macmillan, a U-2 spy plane piloted by a CIA operative named Gary Francis Powers went down over Russia. Although the president had to approve all such flights personally, he allowed the State Department to put out the story that it was an off-course weather plane—the assumption was that Powers would have taken the necessary steps to destroy the plane, and would have committed suicide with the needle available to him. But he had not carried out either of these steps, and by May 11, Eisenhower had to admit the truth, destroying all chances for detente with the Soviets.

After many years of trouble, an island nation became a republic, with Archbishop Makarios as its president. Name the country.

Cyprus, which still has problems that go back to the beginning of the century, due to mixed Greek and Turkish populations, and long dominion by the British.

Two British composers transformed famous works of their country's literature into musical forms, Benjamin Britten making an opera out of a Shakespeare play, and Lionel Bart making a musical out of a Dickens novel. Can you name the opera and the musical?

A Midsummer Night's Dream and *Oliver!*

Which of the following films by major foreign directors went on to be nominated for a Best Foreign Film Oscar?

a. *Last Year at Marienbad,* by Alain Resnais
b. *Rocco and His Brothers,* by Luchino Visconti
c. *La Notte,* by Michelangelo Antonioni

None of them, but for once, this was not Hollywood's fault. Foreign films must first be recommended by their countries of origin and then voted on by a small group of Academy voters who have to sign affidavits that they have seen all the recommended films.

John Updike hit the best-seller lists with a novel whose central character would be the subject of two more novels, the last in 1990. What was the name of the first novel?

Rabbit, Run

The major nonfiction best-seller of the year went behind the scenes to detail the rise and fall of what?

The Rise and Fall of the Third Reich gave the general public a new perspective on Hitler's Nazi regime.

Laurence Durrell published a novel called *Clea.* What was it the final part of?

"The Alexandria Quartet," consisting of the novels *Justine*, *Balthasar*, *Mountolive*, and *Clea*. Lavishly praised and widely read at the time, the "Quartet" has been out of favor for nearly twenty years. But lovers of richly romantic prose will never let it be forgotten entirely.

Arnold Palmer won his first U.S. Open in 1960. How many more would he go on to win?

Surprisingly, none.

Tennis immortal Rod Laver lost the finals of both Wimbledon and the U.S. Open to the same man. What nationality was the winner?

Fellow Australian great Neale Fraser.

1961

"Love Makes the World Go Round." The United States cuts off diplomatic relations with Cuba, the Berlin Wall rises, and the Orient Express makes its final fabled run as a regular passenger train.

British novelist Iris Murdoch offers up *A Severed Head*, John Steinbeck declares *The Winter of Our Discontent*, and Irving Stone weighs in with *The Agony and the Ecstasy*. Mystery fans, theatergoers, and cartoon enthusiasts are saddened by the deaths of Dashiell Hammett, George S. Kaufman, and James Thurber. The aftermath of World War II is relived in the movies *Judgment at Nuremberg* and *Exodus*, but the movie of *West Side Story* cops most of the awards, no thanks to Officer Krupke.

Floyd Patterson defends his heavyweight boxing title against both Ingemar Johansson and Tom McNeely, Bobby Fischer checks in with his fourth consecutive U.S. chess title at the ripe age of seventeen, and the seemingly ageless New York Yankees beat the stuffing out of the Cincinnati Reds in a 4–1 World Series.

On January 18 President Eisenhower broadcast a farewell address to the nation. What surprising warning did he issue?

He warned against the development of what he called "a military-industrial complex," saying that "the potential for the disastrous rise of misplaced power exists and will persist."

What was the Bahia de Cochinos, and how did it prove an embarrassment to President Kennedy?

The Bay of Pigs, in English translation, was the site of a totally misconceived, underequipped, and undermanned invasion of Cuba by anti-Castro Cuban counterrevolutionaries who had been funded and trained by the CIA. Although the disastrous plan had originated with the Eisenhower administration the previous year, the carryover CIA head Allen Dulles and the Joint Chiefs of Staff talked a reluctant President Kennedy into going ahead with it. When the "invasion" turned into a monumental fiasco, Kennedy took full blame for it despite the fact that it had been planned by Eisenhower appointees. The Kennedy administration was less than three months old when this disaster occurred in mid-April.

Name the famous American writer who shot himself to death in 1961.

Nobel Prize winner Ernest Hemingway.

Name the Robert Heinlein novel published in 1961 that was a campus best-seller for years.

Stranger in a Strange Land

Name the posthumous winner of the Nobel Peace Prize for 1961.

Dag Hammarskjöld, the secretary general of the United Nations, who was killed in a plane crash in Zambia that year.

What drug was taken off the market in 1961 and led to the development of strict new regulations for testing drugs in the United States?

Thalidomide, a sleeping potion that caused more than eight thousand children to be born with malformed limbs. It had been on the market, sold without prescription in Europe, since 1957.

What best-selling nonfiction book had a great impact on American awareness of environmental damage by overuse of insecticides?

Rachel Carson's *Silent Spring*

For many years there was an asterisk in the record books next to this man's great 1961 achievement. What was his name, and why was there an asterisk?

Roger Maris hit sixty-one home runs in 1961, surpassing Babe Ruth's supposedly unsurpassable 1927 record of sixty, but then Commissioner Ford Frick declared that there would be an asterisk placed next to the record if Maris did not break it in the 154 games that had constituted the baseball season in 1927—it had been extended to 162 games in 1961. Maris almost didn't make it even so. The pressure was causing his hair to fall out at an alarming rate, and it took him the last eight games to get the necessary two remaining homers. He got the record on the last day of the season off the Red Sox rookie Tracy Stallard. Sports writers felt that the asterisk was unfair, pointing out that the outfield fences at Yankee Stadium were closer in during Ruth's day, and that the rigors of coast-to-coast jet travel in the 1960s were more than debilitating enough to cancel out the longer season. Baseball ultimately removed the asterisk.

Can you name the great all-around football player who was the National Football League's leading scorer for the second year in a row in 1961?

Paul Hornung, who had set an all-time season record of 176 points the year before, could manage only 146 in 1961—no one would do better in the NFL until Mark Mosely of the Washington Redskins got 161 in 1983.

Was Gene Fulmer the Middleweight Boxing Champion of the World in 1961 or was he not?

He was and he wasn't. In all three years he was listed as the National Boxing Association champ, but New York and Massachusetts refused to recognize him, in 1961 going instead with Terry Downes, who was also the recognized champion in Europe. Turmoil was the name of the game.

What American athletic team met with tragedy in a plane crash at the Brussels airport in the winter of 1961?

The entire U.S. figure skating team was killed on its way to the World Championships. Among those lost were men's champion Bradley Lord, coach Maribel Vinson Owen, who had been U.S. ladies' champion nine times in the 1920s and 1930s, and her two daughters, Laurence, who had just succeeded Carol Heiss as ladies' champion, and Maribel, "Jr.," who had just become pairs champion along with her partner, Dudley Richards.

This great baseball player died on July 17, 1961. His nickname was "The Georgia Peach." Why was this ironic? Name him.

He was one of the nastiest critters to ever play the game. His name was "Ty" (Tyrus Raymond) Cobb.

He was one of the most fearsome defensive linemen of the New York Giants during the late fifties and early sixties. However, in his off hours he had a hobby that was far away from football. Name this man and his hobby.

Rosey Grier. His hobby was needlepoint.

Procter & Gamble invented a godsend for new mothers in the early sixties. What was this miracle product?

Pampers disposable diapers. Over thirty million dollars worth were sold in the first three years of production.

Alan Shepard made the first U.S. manned space flight in May of 1961. How long was his space capsule, *Freedom 7*, in outer space?

Fifteen minutes

Can you name the Academy Award–winning song of 1961?

"Moon River"

President John F. Kennedy called for a new government program that young people flocked to join. What was it?

The Peace Corps

Harold Robbins had a huge best-seller in 1961. Name it.

The Carpetbaggers

This legendary singer/actress won her only Grammy Award for Album of the Year in 1961. That same year she was nominated for Best Supporting Actress in the Oscar race. Name her, the recording, and the film.

Judy Garland for *Judy at Carnegie Hall.* The film was *Judgment at Nuremburg.*

This 1961 film was doomed from the very beginning. It's curious, because it was packed with talent in every direction, but moviegoers were not impressed. *The Misfits* was direct-

ed by veteran John Huston, screenplay by Arthur Miller, with a stellar cast of Clark Gable, Marilyn Monroe, Montgomery Clift, Thelma Ritter, and Eli Wallach. The sad thing about this film is that only two of these talents are alive today. Name them.

Eli Wallach and Arthur Miller. Clark Gable died before the movie was released at age fifty-nine in 1960. Marilyn Monroe died in 1962 at thirty-six. Montgomery Clift died in 1966 at forty-six. Thelma Ritter died in 1969 at sixty-four.

Why was New York theater critic Walter Kerr not allowed to review the smash hit comedy of the 1961 season?

Because his wife, Jean Kerr, wrote the play, *Mary, Mary.*

After years of prodding by her friend Truman Capote, this author finally completed her novel about a trial in a small southern town. It became a best-seller and won the Pulitzer Prize. Name her and the book.

Harper Lee wrote *To Kill a Mockingbird.*

"The Andy Griffith Show" was a huge success throughout most of the sixties. The show was set in a fictitious southern town. Name the town. Also, who played the adorable kid on that show?

The town was Mayberry. The kid (Opie) was played by Ronny Howard, who went on to be one of the most successful film directors in Hollywood. His credits include *Splash*, *Cocoon*, *Back to the Future*, and *Backdraft*. Not too bad for the little kid from Mayberry, U.S.A.

From 1961 to 1966, two dramatic doctor shows competed for top television ratings. Name the shows and their stars.

"Ben Casey" was played by Vince Edwards, and "Dr. Kildare" was played by Richard Chamberlain.

With the help of a particularly raucous laugh track, this weekly television show entertained many from 1961 to 1966. The star of the show had four legs. What was it?

A horse named "Mr. Ed."

In the early sixties, Mattel toys produced a doll that took little girls by storm. Her name was Barbie. But as the years rolled by, the children demanded that Barbie have a boyfriend. Mattel was more than happy to oblige. Name her boyfriend.

Ken. Shortly came Midge, Christie, Stacey, Allen, and Skipper. By 1965 Barbie and her friends had grossed over $97 million.

In reaction to young men with long hair, there was a famous billboard put up on highways in many states. What was the slogan?

"Beautify America. Get a haircut."

In the mid-sixties, many a teenage girl would get out the ironing board and do some before-school ironing. It wasn't a skirt or a blouse. What was it?

Her hair. The straight look was in. Curls were out.

Though curls were out, teenage girls needed height for the top of their heads. How did they manage the "height"?

There were three "must do" ways of achieving this desired look. They would roll their top hair with empty twelve-ounce beer cans. (Coke or Pepsi would not do.) Then they would rat (back-comb) it till the hair reached the heavens. The final touch was a half can of Aqua Net hair spray. This process only took a mere two hours. What price beauty.

This actor refused a Best Supporting Actor nomination for 1961's *The Hustler.* Who was he, and why did he refuse?

George C. Scott said he didn't believe in award competitions. The Academy nominated him anyway, but he lost out to George Chakiris in *West Side Story.*

Another young actor, making his extremely successful feature film debut, also was adamant that he not be nominated for Best Supporting Actor, but his reasons were very different. Who was this very talented young heartthrob whose sister was already a star?

Warren Beatty, brother of Shirley MacLaine. Even though *Splendor in the Grass* was his first movie, there was no question that he was as much its star as Natalie Wood, and he wanted to be nominated as Best Actor or not at all. He got his wish, and was not nominated in either category.

For the first time, an actress won the Academy Award for Best Actress for a film made in a foreign language. Name her and the film.

Sophia Loren for *Two Women.*

Two of Hollywood's greatest stars, both of whom died too young, were nominated for Best Supporting Actress and Best Supporting Actor for 1961 for the same movie. Both had been nominated in the Best Actress and Best Actor category previously and lost. Their wrenching performances in this particular movie seemed tailor-made for belated Oscars, but they lost to two vastly lesser-known performers, George Chakiris and Rita Moreno, who won for their performances in the year's Best Picture, *West Side Story.* Name the two superstar losers.

In small but essential roles as witnesses at the Nuremburg trials of the horrors perpetrated by the Nazis, Judy Garland

and Montgomery Clift gave the most searing performances of their lives in *Judgment at Nuremburg*, which was also nominated for Best Picture. Perhaps their performances were too searing—and too closely reflected the pain in their own lives. At showings of the movie across the country, there were always a few people who got up and walked out during either the Garland or Clift sequences—they said they simply could not bear to watch such agony being conveyed by stars they loved. It may be that Hollywood felt the same way—or it may be that Hollywood was sick and tired of the traumas of these two legends and opted instead for the youthful energy of Chakiris and Moreno.

"The Dick Van Dyke Show" premiered in 1961, running through 1966. Can you name the rest of the cast?

Mary Tyler Moore, Richard Deacon, Rose Marie, and Morey Amsterdam.

In 1961 this beloved stage and screen actress "sold out" to television land. It was a waste of her talent, but not to her bank account. On the sitcom she played a maid in a perfect little house in the suburbs. Name her and the show.

Shirley Booth as "Hazel." It lasted for three irritating seasons.

For the first time, codirectors shared the Oscar for Best Picture. Name them and the film.

Robert Wise and Jerome Robbins for *West Side Story*

One of Washington's most powerful men over the past two decades died in office in 1961. What was his name, and what position did he hold?

Representative Sam Rayburn of Texas had proved to be perhaps the most powerful Speaker of the House in history during his twenty years in the job. John McCormack of Massachusetts, an old man himself, was elected to succeed him on the basis of seniority in the Democratic leadership.

Civil rights activists were beaten by white mobs in Alabama. What did these activists call themselves?

"Freedom Riders"

How did the United States finally get U-2 pilot Francis Gary Powers out of the Soviet Union?

He was exchanged for Rudolf Abel, a Soviet spy held by the United Sates.

What happened to Uganda and Tanganyika in 1961?

They gained their independence from Great Britain.

World-renowned dramatists Jean Anouilh and John Osborne had hit plays that focused on famous religious leaders of the twelfth and the sixteenth centuries, respectively. What were the one-word titles of the two plays?

Anouilh's *Becket* focused on the struggle between Saint Thomas à Becket and Henry II of England; Osborne's *Luther* explored the rebellious personality of the Protestant Reformation.

From silent movies to modern times, films were made about Jesus Christ. But we were never allowed to see His face. It was considered blasphemous to portray Him except from the back. But in 1961 Hollywood changed everything around and produced a huge biblical epic that presented Jesus as a flesh-and-blood man. Name the movie and the actor who portrayed Jesus.

King of Kings. Jesus was played by Jeffrey Hunter.

This British-born Hollywood actress had been nominated for Best Supporting Actress for her very first movie role as a flippant maid in 1944. She was then only nineteen. But by the early 1960s, Hollywood had her playing mothers. Although only in her mid-thirties, she played Elvis Presley's mother in 1961, and both Laurence Harvey's and Warren Beatty's mother in 1962. Name this beloved star of stage, screen, and television.

Angela Lansbury, who was nineteen years older than Elvis Presley when they made *Blue Hawaii*, but only twelve years older than Warren Beatty for *All Fall Down*, while Harvey was only three years her junior in *The Manchurian Candidate*. For this last particularly malevolent mother, Miss Lansbury was nominated a third time for Best Supporting Actress.

1962

"Blowin' in the Wind." An assassination attempt is made on Charles de Gaulle, Adolf Eichmann is hanged, and U Thant becomes the secretary-general of the United Nations. It takes three thousand troops to see to it that James Meredith can become the first black to begin classes at the University of Mississippi, and early champion of civil rights Eleanor Roosevelt dies.

Edward Albee wonders *Who's Afraid of Virginia Woolf?*, John Steinbeck wins the Nobel Prize for Literature and publishes a piece of fluff called *Travels with Charlie*, and William Faulkner dies before the publication of his lightest and most humorous novel, *The Reivers*, which will win the Pulitzer Prize the following year.

The Toronto Maple Leafs begin a three-year reign as Stanley Cup Champions, and Sonny Liston knocks out Floyd Patterson in the first round. The Yankees eke out a seesaw 4–3 win over the San Francisco Giants in the World Series.

Linus Pauling had received the Nobel Prize for Chemistry in 1954. What Nobel was he awarded in 1962?

The Peace Prize, in recognition of his work against the use of nuclear weapons. The only other person to win two Nobel Prizes was Marie Curie.

Name the absurdist play by a young Harvard graduate that had a name too long to fit on any theater marquee.

Oh Dad, Poor Dad, Mamma's Hung You in the Closet and I'm Feeling So Sad, by Arthur Kopit.

Name the best-selling novel that followed a number of women who had become friends at college through their postcollege lives.

The Group, by Mary McCarthy

Name the hit movie based on one of the first novels ever written.

Tony Richardson's rambunctious adaptation of Henry Fielding's 1749 masterpiece *Tom Jones*. The movie made an instant star out of Albert Finney and won Oscars for Best Picture, Richardson's directing, John Osborne's screenplay, and John Addison's score.

The most famous art theft of the time was that of the portrait of the Duke of Wellington from the National Gallery in London. As an inside joke, the missing portrait was shown hanging on a wall in the hideaway of the villain in the first of the most successful series of movies ever made. Name the villain (whose name was used as the title of this 1962 movie) and the hero who brought him down.

Dr. No was foiled by James Bond (007).

There was an unusual outcome to baseball's All Star Game in 1962. What was it?

It was the only All Star Game the American League won in the decade.

Henry Mancini had a gift for writing very popular songs for rather grim movies. He did it again this year and won the Oscar for best song. Name this title song.

"Days of Wine and Roses"

This comedy album starring Vaughn Meader had the whole country laughing in 1962. What was it about?

Life at the White House with the Kennedy family.

"The Many Loves of Dobie Gillis" was a television favorite from 1959 to 1963. It starred Dwayne Hickman in the title role. But he had some steady support from two of his costars, Bob Denver (as Maynard G. Krebs) and Tuesday Weld (as Thalia Menninger). Thalia had a boyfriend who caused a lot of conflict. Name the actor who played "the conflict."

Somebody named Warren Beatty. Whatever became of him, nobody knows.

Gregory Peck won Best Actor in 1962 for *To Kill a Mockingbird.* His young costar, Mary Badham, was nominated for Best Supporting Actress. She did not win, but what child actress did in that same year?

Patty Duke for *The Miracle Worker*

A very famous actress placed this ad in *The Daily Variety* in the early sixties: "Mother of three, 10, 11 and 15. Divorcée American. Thirty years experience as an actress in motion pictures. Mobile and more affable than rumor would have it. Wants steady employment in Hollywood. Has also had Broadway experience." Who placed this ad?

Miss Bette Davis. The ad worked. In 1962 she made a stunning comeback in *Whatever Happened to Baby Jane?*

This singing quartet did most certainly keep slow dancing alive in the early sixties. Their recording hits were (to name a few) "Dedicated to the One I Love," "Soldier Boy,"

and "Will You Still Love Me Tomorrow?" What did these girls call themselves?

The Shirelles.

When these two teenagers started their musical act together in the fifties, they called themselves "Tom and Jerry." When the sixties came around, they changed their names. What were the new names?

Simon and Garfunkel

In 1962 two famous women, who were total opposites, teamed up for an evening of song and dance at Carnegie Hall. One was British-born, the other Texas-born. Name them.

Julie Andrews and Carol Burnett. From beginning to end, the two ladies had the audience in the palm of their hands.

In the early sixties, one wouldn't be caught dead without some piece of apparel made of this fabric. It was "guaranteed to bleed." Name this fabric that terrorized mothers for years.

Madras. It did, indeed, bleed. This fabric had to be hand-washed separately. The ironing of a shirt or skirt was no picnic for Mama.

The 1962 musical *No Strings*, with music and lyrics by Richard Rogers, was interesting for several reasons. It was the first show that Rogers did completely on his own after the death of his longtime lyricist, Oscar Hammerstein. The plot revolved around an interracial love affair, which was unusual at that time. The title of the show had a double meaning in that there were no strings in the orchestra. Also, leading lady Diahann Carroll tied for Best Actress in the Tony Award race. Who was the other singing actress?

Anna Maria Alberghetti for *Carnival*

Frank Sinatra was fond of this singing actress, but he once said, "She is technically one of the worst singers in the business." Who was Frankie talking about?

Judy Garland

In 1962 a young actress/singer made her Broadway debut in *I Can Get It for You Wholesale*. She managed to steal the show from its star with her only singing number. Name her.

Barbra Streisand. The star was Elliott Gould, whom she married within the year. The song was "Miss Marmelstein," which she sang while wheeling madly about the stage in an office desk chair.

From the late fifties to the mid-sixties, motion picture musicals were still popular. Deborah Kerr in *The King and I* (1956), Natalie Wood in *West Side Story* (1961), Audrey Hepburn in *My Fair Lady* (1964), all sang their hearts out on-screen. But did they really?

No. Vocals for all three actresses were done by the talented Marni Nixon.

Marilyn Monroe and Charles Laughton both died in 1962. Had they ever played opposite each other on the screen?

Yes, in *O. Henry's Full House* in 1952, an anthology based on five O. Henry stories.

For what 1962 event was a giant television screen installed in Grand Central Station in New York City?

John Glenn's historic orbit of the earth on February 20. He was the first American to do so, but Yuri Gagarin of the Soviet Union had made the first orbital flight in April of 1961.

This man was a football sensation from the University of Colorado in 1939, leading the nation in scoring, rushing, and total offense. The Phi Beta Kappa student became the leading ground-gainer in the NFL as a rookie the next year. He then spent a year at Oxford as a Rhodes scholar. Returning to pro football for the 1940 and 1941 seasons, he then quit football to study law. To what high position did President Kennedy name this athletic and academic whiz in 1962?

Byron "Whizzer" White was appointed an associate justice of the Supreme Court.

This golfer won his second British Open in a row and his third Masters tournament, but he ran into trouble at the U.S. Open. Forced into a play-off, he was beaten by an up-and-coming young man. Name both golfers.

In a fitting confrontation, Jack Nicklaus got his first win in a major tournament in the play-off, the greatest golfer of his generation taking the measure of the greatest golfer of the previous generation. Arnold Palmer would win another Masters title in 1964 and would be the leading money winner in both 1962 and 1963, the latter with the biggest take of his career ($128,230, which now seems measly), but Jack Nicklaus's day was just dawning.

In 1962 the Los Angeles Dodgers had the most honors of any team in baseball. Maury Wills, who broke Ty Cobb's record of 96 stolen bases with 104 for the season, was named MVP; Don Drysdale won the Cy Young award with a twenty-five-game season, and the batting championship in the National League went to Tommy Davis, who had a .346 average and a league-leading 153 RBIs. By how many games did they beat the San Francisco Giants for the pennant?

They didn't. At the end of the season they were tied with the Giants, who won a three-game play-off 2–1. The main reason they didn't make it was that Sandy Koufax was put out of action in mid-July by a circulatory problem in his pitching hand.

Playing for an expansion team that compiled the worst record (40–120) in the history of baseball, this outfielder hit a triple in one game but was called out for not touching either first *or* second base. And this was just another detail in a tapestry of ineptitude. Name the player and his team.

"Marvelous Marv" Thronberry was such a bad player that he became a fan favorite on the fledgling New York Mets, who left Manager Casey Stengel in a state of continual amazement and asking, "Can't anybody here play this game?"

How many days did the Cuban Missile Crisis of 1962 last?

It lasted from October 16 to 28, a total of thirteen days.

A satirical revue on British TV called "That Was the Week That Was" became enormously successful and influenced the creators of such American programs as "Laugh-In" and "The Smothers Brothers Comedy Hour." The brash young host of the British show went on to become a major TV personality on both sides of the Atlantic, but turned increasingly serious as the years went on. Name him.

David Frost, who went from lampooning statesmen to interviewing them one on one.

All the New York City newspapers went on strike beginning December 8, 1962. When did the strike end?

a. January 30
b. March 2
c. April 1

It ended, fittingly enough, on April Fool's Day. In the long hiatus, so many New Yorkers discovered that TV news was all they needed that the nine newspapers began to get their ranks drastically thinned for lack of readers.

What was *Weatherly*, and what did she do to an Australian named *Gretel* in 1962?

The American yacht *Weatherly* successfully defended the America's Cup, beating challenger *Gretel* 4–1.

In 1962 Arnold Palmer was the leading money winner in the PGA. Over among the women, Mickey Wright was the LPGA money leader for the second year in a row. About how many times more money did Palmer win than Wright?

a. About four times as much
b. About six times as much
c. About eight times as much

Somewhat surprisingly, the answer is a. These days the discrepancy is even less, as prize amounts have risen on both sides.

In 1962 Don Carter was both the leading money winner and gained the highest average in what sport?

Hall of Famer Carter was one of the greats of professional bowling. Since bowling became an important TV sport, the money leaders have taken home three to four times as much as the $49,972 Carter earned in 1962, but the leading averages have stayed very much in the vicinity of his 212.844 per match.

The original Broadway cast of *Who's Afraid of Virginia Woolf?* was far different from the eventual movie version,

but perhaps superior. Can you name the original cast?

Uta Hagen as Martha, Arthur Hill as George, Melinda Dillon as Honey, and George Grizzard as Nick.

Frank Loesser and Abe Burrows taught Broadway audiences how to do something in a musical way. What was it?

How to Succeed in Business Without Really Trying. They won a Pulitzer Prize for their efforts.

One of the best-selling books of 1962 was based on a comic strip. Name the book and author.

Happiness Is a Warm Puppy, by Charles M. Schulz, creator of *Peanuts.*

Though she called in sick for too many performances of this Broadway show, she still managed to set the city on fire as Maxine in Tennessee Williams's *Night of the Iguana.* It was not just her vibrant performance but the fact that this fifty-two-year-old actress wore a blouse cut to the navel. Name her.

Bette Davis

On February 14, 1962, exactly the same hour-long program was shown on all three networks. What was it?

First Lady Jacqueline Kennedy's personal tour of the White House. Watched by eighty million viewers, it helped cement the notion of the Kennedy administration as some kind of "Camelot."

1963

"More" (the theme from *Mondo Cane*). The dalliance between Britain's minister of war, John Profumo, and Christine Keeler forces the resignation of Prime Minister Harold Macmillian, riots against civil rights activists led by Martin Luther King in Birmingham, Alabama, cause President Kennedy to call out three thousand troops, and the government of South Vietnam is overthrown in a military coup. President Kennedy is assassinated in Dallas on November 22, and the supposed assassin, Lee Harvey Oswald, is in turn shot dead by Jack Ruby. Could this be a conspiracy?

John Updike and Iris Murdoch turn mythical with their respective novels *The Centaur* and *The Unicorn*, and Hannah Arendt causes an uproar by trying to discern realities in her book *Eichmann in Jerusalem: A Report on the Banality of Evil.*

For the third year in a row, the New York Giants lose the NFL play-off game, this time to the Chicago Bears, 14–10. Jim "Ball Four" Bouton wins twenty-one games for the Yankees in his second year in the majors, but the Dodgers crush his team 4–0 in the World Series.

On April 9, 1963, he became the first honorary citizen of the United States. Name him.

Sir Winston Churchill.

What new communication device was installed in the White House in 1963?

The hot line, from the White House to the Kremlin.

What happened to Cardinal Montini in 1963?

He was elected to succeed Pope John XXIII and took the name Paul VI.

There was much competition about who would play John F. Kennedy in the film *PT 109*. Who landed the role, and why?

Cliff Robertson. The president hand-picked him.

Hattie McDaniel won the Best Supporting Actress Award for *Gone With the Wind* in 1939. It took twenty-four years for another black star to take home a gold statue. Name him, and the movie.

Sidney Poitier for Best Actor in *Lilies of the Field* in 1963.

In 1963 John Wayne had a cancerous lung removed. He came back strong from that and went on to win a Best Actor Academy Award for *True Grit* in 1969, continuing to make movies into the mid-sixties. But then cancer struck again and he died of it in 1979. What was more, it became apparent as the years went on that cancer was striking a large number of the cast and crew of his 1956 movie about Genghis Khan, *The Conqueror*. Of his costars in that film, Agnes Moorehead died of lung cancer in 1974, and Susan Hayward of brain cancer in 1976. Many lesser-known actors and technicians involved with the film also developed cancer. To what was this coincidence attributed?

The movie had been made in Utah, and unknowingly the cast and crew spent weeks in the vicinity of a former atomic test site that was still a government secret.

John Lewis, Milt Jackson, Percy Heath, and Connie Kay constituted the most popular jazz group of the 1960s. What were they know as?

The Modern Jazz Quartet.

In the late fifties and into the early sixties, The Dave Brubeck Quartet kept us musically calm while rock was screaming its head off. Name the Brubeck album that was called "the relax record."

Take Five

What common fruit, when the inner skin was scraped off and heated in an oven, produced a good high in place of marijuana? Name the fruit. And did this tedious process really work?

The banana. And no, it did not work, though many said it did. A desperate case of mind over matter?

Drug abuse ran rampant in the sixties. The grand guru of LSD, Timothy Leary, came up with a slogan that too many young people took to heart. What was it?

"Tune in, turn on, drop out."

On November 22, 1963, an attorney representing the Pepsi-Cola company flew out of Dallas, Texas, on a flight to New York about two and a half hours before President Kennedy arrived to make the fatal ride past the Texas Book Depository. Who was this fledgling corporate lawyer and former high government official?

Richard M. Nixon

The only film of the actual assassination of President John F. Kennedy was an 18.24-second motion picture sequence

taken by a Dallas garment manufacturer. Name him.

Abraham Zapruder. He had, in fact, forgotten to bring his camera with its Zoomar lens to the office that morning, but his secretary insisted he go home and get it.

How many Americans died in Vietnam while President Kennedy was in office?

a. 700
b. 1,700
c. 75

The answer is c.

Vice President Lyndon B. Johnson refused to be sworn in as president following John F. Kennedy's assassination until what occurred?

LBJ insisted that Jacqueline Kennedy be at his side as he took the oath of office. Because it was widely known that he was unhappy as vice president and that he and Robert Kennedy couldn't stand each other, he was extremely concerned that the president's widow be standing alongside him as he took over the leadership of the country. The fact that the assassination had taken place in his home state of Texas made the situation all the more important, as far as he was concerned—he was fearful that there would be suggestions that he had had something to do with President Kennedy's murder, and indeed, such whispers began almost immediately. It was explained to Mrs. Kennedy that it was vital to the country that she be present, and she agreed to do so, standing with lowered head and stricken eyes in the pink suit splattered with her husband's blood.

Marilyn Monroe was fired from her last uncompleted film, *Something's Got to Give* for reasons of habitual tardiness. The movie was renamed and a new actress was

brought in to replace Miss Monroe. Name the new title and the new actress.

Move Over, Darling. The actress was Doris Day.

This young actor came to national attention as Rowdy Yates on the television series "Rawhide," which ran from 1959 to 1966. He later went on to international fame as a movie star. Name him.

Clint Eastwood

This young singer from Brooklyn won a Grammy Award for her first solo album. On this album, she sang of tears and happy days. Name her.

Barbra Streisand. The hit songs of that album were "Cry Me a River" and "Happy Days Are Here Again."

There was something unique about the 1963 Rose Bowl game between Southern California and Wisconsin. There had never been a game to equal it in one particular way before, and there hasn't been one since. What made it special?

It was the highest-scoring game in the history of the Rose Bowl, with Southern California defeating Wisconsin 42–37.

Lionel Taylor accomplished something he had done every year since the founding of the American Football League in 1960. What was it?

The Denver Bronco wide receiver led the new league in pass-receptions. As of 1989, he still ranked twelfth among all receivers in either the NFL or AFL, with 7,195 yards as a career total.

This nineteen-year-old regained the U.S. Championship of a very demanding but almost motionless sport that he

had first won when he was fourteen. Name him.

Bobby Fischer had reigned as U.S. Chess Champion from 1957 to 1961. Larry Evans held the title for 1961–62, and Fischer would now be the champion through 1968, and go on to become World Champion in 1972.

In 1963 this basketball player on the NBA's dominant team was voted MVP for the third year in a row. Name him.

The incomparable Bill Russell of the Boston Celtics, who had also won the award in 1958 and would do so again in 1965. Only Kareem Abdul-Jabbar would ever equal Russell in MVP wins, and even he couldn't do it three years in a row. Although there are many players ahead of him on the all-time scoring lists, only Wilt Chamberlain had more rebounds than Russell's 21,620, and not even Chamberlain could get the ball to another player faster than Russell. From his college days at San Francisco University to his Gold Medal performance in the 1956 Olympics down through his entire pro career, there was never a more selfless player or better team leader.

A National League second baseman was named Rookie of the Year in 1963. Name him.

Pete Rose.

Can you name the Academy Award–winning song of 1963?

No reflection on Mr. Rose, but the song was "Call Me Irresponsible."

Can you guess the number one best-selling single of 1963?

"Dominique," as sung by "The Singing Nun."

In this 1963 movie, Jimmy Durante was in a car accident. Before his character died, he gave a clue to where a huge fortune was buried. Then he literally kicked a bucket down a hill. Name this very funny movie.

Stanley Kramer's *It's a Mad, Mad, Mad, Mad World*

In 1963, on ABC, the TV would suddenly turn "snowy" for a short period of time. Through the snow, we heard these words: "There is nothing wrong with your television set. Do not adjust the picture. We are controlling transmission." What was this all about?

The very clever introduction to the science fiction series "The Outer Limits." Like Orson Welles's famous radio presentation "The War of the Worlds," it scared people for a while.

This 1963 TV series, starring George C. Scott, lasted only two seasons. It dealt with serious urban problems, which didn't sit too well with Dad, Mom, and the kids. It also had a black female costar in a noncomic role. In other words, she didn't play a maid. Name the show and the future Emmy Award–winning actress.

"East Side/West Side." The actress was the very gifted Cicely Tyson.

A baseball player with great talents and a nose for trouble won National League Rookie of the Year honors in 1963. His teammates disliked him, however, and gave him a nickname that he insisted on taking as a compliment. Who was he, and what was the nickname that stuck with him throughout his career?

The cheeky and aggressive Pete Rose was called "Charlie Hustle" by Cincinnati Reds teammates who thought he was entirely too full of himself.

Jimmy Piersall of the Boston Red Sox never felt that his abilities were properly appreciated, especially by the press. On the occasion of his one hundredth home run, what did he do to make sure the press paid attention?

He trotted down to first and all the way around the bases going backward.

Name the navy quarterback who won the Heisman trophy in 1963.

One of the all-time greats, named Roger Staubach.

This artist was given a show at the Guggenheim Museum in New York City in 1963. Many people scoffed, but he was taken seriously for more than fifteen minutes. Name him.

Andy Warhol.

British writer Jessica Mitford caused an uproar with her best-selling exposé of what grim American business?

The American Way of Death lacerated the American funeral business.

Stanley Kubrick made us laugh at the end of the world in his 1963 movie. Name it.

Dr. Strangelove or How I Learned to Stop Worrying and Love the Bomb.

Great Britain's bid to join the Common Market was rejected because of the objections of one man. Name him.

Charles de Gaulle, who never was very good at being grateful to the British for naming him head of the Free French during World War II.

1964

"A Hard Day's Night." Jack Ruby is convicted of killing Lee Harvey Oswald, and the Warren Commission says Oswald had acted alone. President Johnson and the military brass lie to the country about an attack on a U.S. destroyer in order to get Congress to pass the Tonkin Gulf resolution, escalating the war in Vietnam. Race riots break out in several American cities.

Eric Berne publishes *Games People Play*, Arthur Miller exploits his onetime wife Marilyn Monroe in *After the Fall*, and Ernest Hemingway takes nasty swipes at F. Scott Fitzgerald in the posthumously published memoir *A Movable Feast*. Richard Hofstadter wins the Pulitzer Prize for nonfiction for *Anti-Intellectualism in American Life*.

Arnold Palmer wins his fourth Masters tournament in seven years, but Jack Nicklaus is the top money winner. The Yankees fail to eke out a win over the St. Louis Cardinals in a seven-game Series.

Who coined the phrase "global village"?

Canadian writer Marshall McLuhan, whose reflections on the media also brought forth the statement "The medium is the message."

Name the tap-dancing senator, elected in 1964, who had starred with the likes of Judy Garland, Shirley Temple, and Margaret O'Brien in movies of the 1930s and 1940s.

Senator George Murphy of California

This seventeen-year-old became the first person ever to break the two-minute barrier in two-hundred-meter freestyle swimming. Name him.

Don Schollander, who went on to break the world or Olympic record in every event he entered at the Tokyo Olympics of 1964, bringing home four Gold Medals.

This Australian woman swimmer went for her third consecutive Olympic Gold Medal in the Hundred Meter Freestyle. Who was she, and did she make it?

Dawn Fraser not only won for the third time in twelve years, but got her best time of all: 59.5 seconds.

At the age of twenty-two, a Gold Medalist at the 1960 Olympics became boxing's Heavyweight Champion of the World. Meanwhile a future rival was winning a Gold Medal in the 1964 Olympics in Tokyo. What were the names of both boxers, and did they win their respective Gold Medals in the same Olympic weight categories?

Cassius Clay (who changed his name that same year to Muhammad Ali after becoming a Black Muslim) became the second youngest Heavyweight Champion in boxing history. In the 1960 Olympics, Clay/Ali had fought in the Light Heavyweight division, while his future rival, Joe Frazier, won in the Super Heavyweight division in 1964. Now known as Muhammad Ali, the champion was stripped of his title in 1967 after refusing the draft on religious grounds. His draft case went all the way to the Supreme Court, and was decided in his favor in 1971. But on his return to the ring, he was defeated by Joe Frazier. He regained the title in 1974 from George Foreman, the 1968 Olympic Super Heavyweight Gold Medalist, then lost and regained it from Leon Spinks in 1978. Spinks had been the 1976 Gold Medalist in the Light Heavyweight division of the Olympics. Ali lost the title for the final time to Larry Holmes in 1980, but is the only man to hold the title three separate times.

One of the great middle-distance runners of all time, a New Zealander, won his second Olympic Gold Medal in a row in the Eight-Hundred-Meter Run and added a Gold in the Fifteen-Hundred-Meter Run. Name him.

Peter Snell

Their first names were Ludmilla and Oleg, and they were to become legends in their sport. Who were they, and what did they do?

Ludmilla Beloussova and Oleg Protopopov won the first of two successive Gold Medals in Pairs Figure Skating in 1964. They subsequently married and continued to be regarded with awe when they skated right on through the 1980s. They established a standard that has been matched but never exceeded, a standard called perfection.

An imperfect world was confronted with a television commercial during the 1964 presidential campaign that showed a little girl pulling petals off a daisy. Why did this cause justifiable outrage in the camp of Republican presidential nominee Barry Goldwater?

The commercial ended with an atomic bomb going off behind the little girl, a not-so-subtle message that Senator Goldwater could be expected to start a nuclear war. The ad was withdrawn in rapid order.

The Twenty-fourth Amendment to the Constitution was adopted in 1964. What did it abolish?

The poll tax, which had been used in many states to keep poor blacks from voting.

Who was convicted of fraud and conspiracy as a result of the efforts of Attorney General Robert Kennedy?

Teamster boss Jimmy Hoffa

In 1964 there was another sensational new play with a very long title, totaling twenty-seven words. It was set in an insane asylum. Name it.

Marat/Sade (The Persecution and Assassination of Jean-Paul Marat as Performed by the Inmates of the Asylum of Charenton under the Direction of the Marquis de Sade), by Peter Weiss. The intense and brilliantly original Peter Brook production was filmed by the director in 1966 and brought Glenda Jackson to worldwide attention.

Who taught Alan Bates to dance in one of the year's hit movies?

Anthony Quinn as *Zorba the Greek.*

For the first Beatles "live" performance on "The Ed Sullivan Show," the studio could only seat 728 people. How many fans requested tickets?

a. Twenty thousand
b. Fifty thousand
c. Seventy thousand

The answer is b. The pandemonium that ensued is amusingly recounted in the 1978 movie *I Wanna Hold Your Hand.*

How much did Ed Sullivan pay the Beatles for appearing on his show three weeks in a row?

a. $2,400 per show
b. $3,500 per show
c. $5,000 per show

The answer is a, which was less than half his going rate for major attractions. But although he got them cheap, seventy-three million watched the first appearance of February 4, 1964, and a phenomenon was launched.

She was replaced because of illness as Bette Davis's costar in the 1964 film *Hush, Hush, Sweet Charlotte* by Olivia De Havilland. Who was this ill actress?

Joan Crawford. The producers were furious about it because of the very profitable pairing of Davis and Crawford in *Whatever Happened To Baby Jane*. However, Miss Davis and Miss De Havilland shed not one salty tear between them for the loss.

Agnes Moorehead was nominated for Best Supporting Actress for her fine work in *Hush, Hush, Sweet Charlotte* but lost out to Lila Kedrova in *Zorba the Greek*. When asked about the Davis/De Havilland/Crawford mess, Miss Moorehead came up with the perfect answer. What was it?

"No comment"

This Frank D. Gilroy play about a troubled veteran's relationship with his parents would go on to win the Pulitzer Prize for Drama and run for nearly two years on Broadway. Name it.

The Subject Was Roses, which also made a star of Martin Sheen and brought Jack Albertson a Tony and later an Oscar as Best Supporting Actor.

The top acting Oscars for 1964 were full of irony. The Best Actor and Best Actress had thrilled Broadway playing opposite each other in a long-running musical comedy hit. The man was given the Oscar for repeating his role in that musical. The actress won for a totally different movie,

having been denied her Broadway role because she wasn't a movie star. Name both winners and the movie star who played opposite the Best Actor winner in the movie.

Rex Harrison and Julie Andrews, who had originated the lead roles in *My Fair Lady* on Broadway, were reunited in postceremony photographs, he winning for the movie of *My Fair Lady*, she for the bigger box-office hit, *Mary Poppins*. Audrey Hepburn had been cast opposite Harrison in the role of Eliza Doolittle, and although she had acted it splendidly, her songs had to be dubbed. She had not even been nominated. But there were no hard feelings between Miss Hepburn and Miss Andrews—Audrey Hepburn had tried to persuade the producers that they were crazy not to cast Julie Andrews in the first place, and Julie and Audrey also posed together for photographers on Oscar night.

This beloved character actress made her last motion picture appearance in 1964. The film was *Mary Poppins*. Name her.

Jane Darwell. Although she had no lines, she managed to charm audiences by just feeding the birds, sitting on the steps of St. Paul in London. Miss Darwell is best known for her Academy Award–winning performance as Ma Joad in *The Grapes of Wrath*.

This 1964 prime-time soap opera was such a hit that it was presented twice a week, as television viewers could not possibly wait a full week to find out what was going to happen next. It also introduced two young future movie stars. Name them and the series.

Mia Farrow and Ryan O'Neal. This drama was entitled "Peyton Place." A little town, nice to grow up in.

This 1955 Oscar winner won fresh national popularity on his own weekly television series that provided laughs on the high seas. Name the actor and the series.

Ernest Borgnine in "McHale's Navy"

The title song from *Hello Dolly* was recorded by many famous vocalists. But who turned it into a number one best-selling single?

None other than Louis "Satchmo" Armstrong.

In 1964 *Fiddler on the Roof* opened to somewhat lukewarm reviews. To this day the show is running all around the world. Who, if any, were not in the original Broadway cast?

a. Bette Midler
b. Austin Pendelton
c. Julia Migenes
d. Bert Convy
e. Bea Arthur

The answer is a; Bette Midler joined the cast as a replacement.

One Tuesday night in 1964, this sitcom garnered 65 percent of the television viewing audience. Name the show and the down home actors who appeared in it.

"The Beverly Hillbillies." The cast included Irene Ryan, Buddy Ebsen, Max Baer, Jr., and Donna Douglas.

In 1964 the much-awaited "Judy Garland Show" was given the toughest time slot on Sunday nights. What was she up against?

"Bonanza," which constantly outgunned her. Miss Garland's show died in one season.

This beloved American comedian ended his weekly television show by saying, "Good night, Mrs. Calabash,

wherever you are." What was his name, and who was Mrs. Calabash?

Jimmy Durante. As for Mrs. Calabash, nobody knows.

In her long television career, Carol Burnett ended her shows by pulling on her right earlobe. What did this mean?

It was saying hello to her grandmother, who raised her.

This children's book author had his first great success at the end of the 1950s. Between 1960 and 1964 he published four more books that, like two earlier ones, are among the fifteen top-selling children's books in the history of American publishing. Name this whimsical author.

Dr. Seuss, the pseudonymn for Theodor Geisel. His fame began in 1957 with *The Cat in the Hat*. During the early sixties, *Green Eggs and Ham; One Fish, Two Fish, Red Fish, Blue Fish; Hop on Pop*; and *Dr. Seuss's ABC* rocketed out of the bookstores.

Whimsey of another kind was available in book form to Beatles fans. What was the name of the book, and who wrote it?

In His Own Write was John Lennon's first book.

Soft-porn whimsey made the best-seller list in a novel by Terry Southern and Mason Hoffenberg. Name the book.

Candy

From 1964 to 1966, two very, very strange families on different TV shows charmed us with unending lunacy. They were not quite of this world. Name the shows.

"The Munsters" and "The Addams Family."

Name the beloved comedienne who said good night for the last time in 1964.

Gracie Allen, who, when husband George Burns asked her to "say good night, Gracie," always replied, with her inimitable logic, "Good night, Gracie."

How many days did Elizabeth Taylor wait to marry Richard Burton after her divorce from Eddie Fisher?

a. Ten days
b. Three days
c. Seventeen days

The answer is a.

British playwrights had a banner year in 1964. Connect the plays listed below in the left-hand column with the correct playwright in the right-hand column.

1. *Inadmissible Evidence*	a. Harold Pinter
2. *Homecoming*	b. Peter Shaffer
3. *The Royal Hunt of the Sun*	c. John Osbourne

1, c; 2, a; 3, b. All three were subsequently New York as well as London successes.

The British were greatly alarmed by what was called "the Brain Drain." Did this have to do with the increasing violence between youths who were divided into two camps called Mods and Rockers, or with something else?

It had to do with the large number of British scientists emigrating to the United States, where they could earn much higher salaries. The violence between Mods and Rockers was another, but rather different, cause for concern.

Whose quatercentenary was celebrated in England?
Shakespeare's

At the Tokyo Summer Olympics, the USSR won forty-one gold medals. Was this four, seven, or nine more than the United States?
It was four more.

In the movie comedy *Walk, Don't Run*, partially filmed during the Tokyo Olympics, the leading man found himself inadvertently taking part in one of the more unusual Olympic events—the Heel-and-Toe Walk. Name the Hollywood superstar who made the most of this difficult but basically hilarious track and field event.
Cary Grant

Who was Sjoukje Dijkstra, and what did she accomplish in 1964?
This young woman from the Netherlands won her third straight World Championship and also took the Gold Medal in Women's Figure Skating at the Winter Olympics.

1965

"King of the Road." Martin Luther King leads four thousand civil rights demonstrators on a march from Selma to Montgomery, Alabama. Adlai Stevenson dies on a trip to London, where the 750th anniversary of the Magna Carta is being celebrated. More than four thousand are arrested during riots in the Watts section of Los Angeles, and demonstrations against the war in Vietnam become numerous.

Frank Marcus has theater audiences agog with *The Killing of Sister George*, and Norman Mailer writes a serial for *Esquire* about a murderous husband. Poet Robert Lowell publishes *The Union Dead*, and Robin Moore celebrates *The Green Berets*. According to Frank Sinatra, "It Was a Very Good Year."

For the first time since 1958, Willie Shoemaker is not the leading money winner in thoroughbred racing, with Braulio Baeza beginning a four-year rein at the top of the list. The Yankees collapse due to injuries, and the Los Angeles Dodgers beat the Minnesota Twins 4–3 in the World Series.

President Lyndon Johnson began to put his "Great Society" programs into place with the signing of the original Medicare bill. Was this program Johnson's idea?

No, it had been proposed by President Kennedy in 1960, when he was running for the office. One of the reasons he was unable to get it through Congress was that by choosing L.B.J. as his vice president, he had lost a majority leader in the Senate who was a past master at arm twisting. Now in the Oval Office as an elected president, Johnson was able to get back to putting on the pressure the way he had as majority leader.

Name the Black Muslim leader killed by gunfire in New York City while giving a speech.

Malcolm X was ironically the victim of his old radical friends. Having converted to the Muslim religion and turned away from his advocacy of violence against whites, he was seen as a traitor to the cause.

What did Aleksei Leonov and Edward White both do in 1965?

The Soviet and American astronauts both left their space capsules for a walk.

This outsize actor won three Tony Awards within four years from 1961 to 1965, two as Best Actor in a musical and one as Best Actor in a play. Name him.

Zero Mostel. He won for *A Funny Thing Happened on the Way to the Forum* in 1963, *Fiddler on the Roof* in 1965, and *Rhinoceros* in 1961.

Name the miracle sweetener used in soft drinks in the mid sixties.

Cyclamate. It was later discovered that it caused cancer.

In November of 1965, a power failure blacked out major areas of the Northwest, leaving thirty million people fumbling in the dark. What showed a considerable increase the following year that was attributed to the blackout?

The birth rate was significantly higher nine months later.

In the mid-sixties, it was difficult to go anywhere without seeing this artist's paintings and posters in bright Day-Glo

colors. He practically brought the word *psychedelic* into our everyday language. Name the artist.

Peter Max

This Broadway matinee idol of the fifties and sixties was the son of the most famous comedian in silent film history. Name him and his father.

Sydney Chaplin, son of Charlie Chaplin. He starred opposite Judy Holliday in *Bells Are Ringing*, Barbra Streisand in *Funny Girl*, and Carole Lawrence in *Subways Are for Sleeping*.

"It is sobering to consider that when Mozart was my age, he had already been dead for a year." What satirical songwriter/performer used this in his act?

Tom Lehrer

In the mid-sixties, posters decorated many a dorm room. One of the first to go up was a still of a famous actor from the 1940s who had become a hero to a new generation. Name him.

Humphrey Bogart. The still was from *Casablanca.*

The leading lady and title character of this Broadway show became the youngest ever to win a musical Best Actress Tony, and went on to become a superstar. Name her and the show.

Liza Minnelli wowed New York audiences as *Flora the Red Menace* at the age of nineteen. This show began her career-long association with songwriters John Kander and Fred Ebb.

Name the character actor, still going strong in 1991, who took Broadway by storm and went on to win a Tony Award

for Best Actor for a one-man show.

Hal Holbrook in *Mark Twain Tonight!* Only forty at the time, Holbrook presented a white-haired Twain in his sixties looking back on his life.

In the spring of 1965, two American singer/composers, famous for their protest songs, one male, the other female, made a tour of England that was the subject of the documentary *Don't Look Back.* Name the singers.

Bob Dylan and Joan Baez

This "tag line" quickly made its way into our everyday speech, thanks to a weekly sitcom. The line was "Would you believe . . . ?" Name the show and the actor who starred.

"Get Smart," starring Don Adams. The show ran from 1965 to 1970.

The television sitcom "My Mother, the Car" was thought by most to be the worst thing to ever hit nighttime viewing. However, there was something interesting about this show. Can you think what it might have been?

The voice of the car was supplied by veteran movie and television actress Ann Sothern.

In the mid-sixties, a popular black stand-up comic put his career on hold and got deeply involved in political activism. He even ran for president in 1968 on the Peace and Freedom party ticket. Name him.

Dick Gregory.

Which of the following ladies did *not* play Dolly Levi in the Broadway musical *Hello Dolly*?

a. Betty Grable
b. Ginger Rogers

c. Pearl Bailey
d. Shirley Booth
e. Martha Raye

The answer is d.

Walter Matthau played Oscar Madison, the slob, in Neil Simon's 1965 smash hit comedy, *The Odd Couple*. But who played his immaculate roommate, Felix Ungar?

Art Carney. Jack Lemmon replaced him in the film version.

In 1965 this actor played Captain von Trapp in the Oscar-winning best picture *The Sound of Music*. Who was the actor, and what did *he* call the movie?

Christopher Plummer. He referred to the film as *The Sound of Mucus*.

Richard Harris portrayed King Arthur in the film version of the musical *Camelot*. How did he refer to the name of that film?

Camelsnot. After this 1966 film, he obviously changed his mind. Mr. Harris toured his *Camelsnot*, in a theatrical production, all over the nation.

In London Vanessa Redgrave won a Best Actress award in a play based on a novel by Muriel Spark. When it subsequently opened in New York, Zoe Caldwell won a Tony in the same role, and Maggie Smith would eventually win an Oscar in the part. Name this terrific title role.

The Prime of Miss Jean Brodie, by Jay Presson Allen.

Can you name the entertainer who has been awarded more honors by the United States than any other civilian?

Bob Hope

The *New York Times* wrote about this famous model, "Looks like your next door neighbor, if he happens to be a skinny 12-year-old boy." Name the boy.

Her name was (and is) Twiggy.

By the mid-sixties, many Americans went diet-crazy. Name the product that encouraged people to lose all that flab.

Metrecal

In 1965 a new soft drink was developed to prevent heat exhaustion in athletes. What was this breakthrough drink?

Gatorade

Who was Spain's world-famous "beatnik of the bull-ring"?

El Cordobes, who wore his hair in a Beatle-like cut, outraged bullfighting purists with his clowning around, but became the richest and most famous bullfighter of his era.

Name the Ivy League basketball player who was named the outstanding player at the NCAA finals and was awarded the 1965 Sullivan Award as the outstanding amateur athlete of the year.

Bill Bradley of Princeton, now U.S. senator from New Jersey. Although the Princeton team lost the finals to UCLA 91–80, Bradley shone. He then went to Oxford as a Rhodes scholar before joining the New York Knicks for a sterling pro career.

The New York Yankee 1965 season was a disaster. Which of the following Yankee players was *not* sidelined with

injuries for at least fifty games?

a. Roger Maris
b. Mickey Mantle
c. Joe Pepitone
d. Tony Kubek
e. Elston Howard

The answer is Joe Pepitone, but he didn't get along with new manager Johnny Keane and had a terrible year. Maris played in only 43 games, Mantle in 108, Kubek in 93, and Howard in 102.

In the 1960s two eventual Hall of Fame pitchers on different National League teams were twice named Most Valuable Player in the World Series. Name them.

Sandy Koufax of the Los Angeles Dodgers won the Sport Magazine award in 1963 and 1965. Bob Gibson of the St. Louis Cardinals won in 1964 and 1967.

This great running back led the NFL in rushing for the third consecutive year. Name him.

Jim Brown of the Cleveland Browns racked up 1,544 yards and scored seventeen touchdowns.

This young superstar-to-be made her first solo TV musical special in 1965. It was filmed entirely in the very grand Bergdorf Goodman store in New York City. Name her and the name of the show.

Barbra Streisand. The name of her special was "My Name Is Barbra."

This popular black comedian kept us in stitches via his recordings. But he really came to national attention when he teamed up with Robert Culp in an espionage adventure series. Name him and the show.

Bill Cosby in "I Spy"

Before they became famous, The Beatles fired their drummer, Peter Best, and hired Ringo Starr to replace him. They later sued Best. Why?

Mr. Best came out with an album entitled *Best of The Beatles*, thus confusing record buyers. He did not get away with his misrepresentation.

"He's the sexiest man on TV." What veteran screen actress made this comment about Robert Wagner?

Bette Davis

This was a banner year in the Oscar race for Best Picture. Nominated were: *The Sound of Music*, *Darling*, *Dr. Zhivago*, *Ship of Fools*, and *A Thousand Clowns*. Which film won the gold statue?

Although *Dr. Zhivago* waltzed away with many awards, producer Robert Wise hummed his way up to the podium to accept the gold for *The Sound of Music*. The sound of money? Yes.

Julie Christie's Oscar as Best Actress for *Darling* was boosted by the fact that she also starred in *Dr. Zhivago*. But, in fact, the young beauty, virtually unknown a year earlier, also had a third movie released in 1965, in which she costarred with Rod Taylor. Can you name it?

Young Cassidy, based on the early manhood of Irish playwright Sean O'Casey.

Ralph Nader had a best-selling book that gave Detroit executives incipient apoplexy. What was the title of the book?

Unsafe at Any Speed

President Johnson, knowing that Arthur Goldberg was not entirely happy as a Supreme Court justice, persuaded him to resign and appointed him ambassador to the United Nations. He told Goldberg that his talents were absolutely essential to the UN job. But what was Johnson's real reason?

He wanted to appoint his longtime crony Abe Fortas to the Supreme Court. Fortas was brilliant but slippery, and eventually had to resign from the Court because of a conflict-of-interest financial scandal.

Since 1950 both AP and UPI sportswriters had been polled about the rankings of the top college football teams. What happened at the end of the season for the first time in 1965?

The two polls came up with different answers, with the AP choosing Alabama, and UPI selecting Michigan State. Everybody was unhappy.

This Chicago Black Hawks left wing was named pro hockey's Most Valuable Player in 1965, and was also awarded the Lady Byng Trophy for Most Gentlemanly Player—an unusual parlay. Name this hockey immortal.

Bobby Hull, who played with the Black Hawks from 1957 to 1972, scoring a total of 610 goals. He was the league's leading scorer in 1960 and 1962, and was named MVP for a second year in a row in 1966.

1966

"Strangers in the Night." The Soviet and American spacecraft *Luna 9* and *Surveyor 1* both land on the moon, and Edwin Aldrin spends more than two hours outside *Gemini 12* while in orbit. After years of international fund-raising, the temples of Abu Simbel in Egypt are moved to save them from being submerged by the waters created by the Aswan Dam. Indira Gandhi becomes the prime minister of India, and de Gaulle begins his second term as president of France.

The musical *Man of La Mancha* transports theatergoers to another time, while *On a Clear Day You Can See Forever* tries to haul them back in time by the scruff of the neck. A little red book called *Quotations of Chairman Mao* becomes a campy success on college campuses, not exactly what Mao had in mind.

Francis Chichester completes his 107-day solo voyage from London to Sydney, Australia, and Jim Ryun sets a new world record for running the mile. Led by two greats named Robinson, Frank and Brooks, the Baltimore Orioles overwhelm the lackluster Los Angeles Dodgers 4–0 in the World Series.

Why were the people of Spain outraged at the United States in 1966?

An American B-52 crashed off the coast of Spain, dropping three unarmed hydrogen bombs on land and one in the ocean.

This politician, who had lost a senate race in 1964, became the first Republican ever elected to the House from Houston. Who was he?

George Bush. He served two terms in the House before

being appointed ambassador to the United Nations by President Nixon.

What new look in women's fashion, originating in London, became popular in 1966?

The miniskirt, pushed by designer Mary Quant.

Name the cosmetic queen who died in 1966.

Elizabeth Arden.

"It could have been the put-on of the century. Just imagine the headlines in the newspapers and magazines: ACTUAL ALIEN AGREES TO APPEAR IN SCIENCE FICTION TV SERIES." Who wrote these words?

Leonard Nimoy wrote these words in 1975 as he looked back on the creation of the character of Mr. Spock on "Star Trek." He was initially so concerned that the character might turn out to be ludicrous that he considered disguising himself to the extent that no one would know he was a serious actor named Leonard Nimoy, and joked about pretending to actually be an alien. But audiences fell in love with Mr. Spock at first sight when the initial episode aired on September 8, 1966. The problem after "Star Trek" ended its modestly successful run four years later was for Nimoy to get audiences to accept him as anyone other than Spock. It took a while, but when he got splendid reviews as a replacement star of Broadway's long-running *Equus* in the late 1970s, Nimoy knew the problem was behind him for good.

Name the bizarre 1966 movie based on a comic strip that starred Monica Vitti in the title role, and had a pop art look.

Modesty Blaise

The title of a 1966 movie referred to the temperature at which paper burns. Name the movie, the director, and the author of the novel from which it was derived.

Fahrenheit 451 was directed by François Truffaut and based on the novel by Ray Bradbury.

Who was Frodo Baggins?

The hero of J.R.R. Tolkien's three-volume fantasy *The Lord of the Rings*, which had originally been published in 1953–54, but which caught on in a big way among college students in 1966 and became a top paperback best-seller.

Name the movie that gave Dionne Warwick one of her greatest Burt Bacharach hits.

Alfie, which also made Michael Caine a major star.

This distinguished British actress, who made her reputation playing Shakespearean roles, had a huge impact on a popular television series from 1966 to 1969. Besides being beautiful and very talented, she had an unusual skill for a woman at that time. Name her, the character she played, the show, and her special skill.

Diana Rigg played Mrs. Emma Peel on "The Avengers." Mrs. Peel could bring a three-hundred-pound man to the floor by way of karate.

Another British import, Angela Lansbury, won Tony Awards for the musicals *Mame, Dear World, Gypsy,* and *Sweeney Todd.* But her first outing in a musical was a total flop. Name the show.

Anyone Can Whistle, by Stephen Sondheim. The show ran for one week in New York City.

Designer Rudi Gernreich caused quite a scandal with his new line of women's swimwear. What was all the controversy about?

The bathing suits were topless, held up by two small straps crisscrossing the breasts. His idea was a bust and quickly faded.

The mid-sixties went fad-crazy, mostly via the British, what with the mini and the midi. The "Brits" instructed us Americans to put something else on the body. What was it?

Body paint. Green and pink striped legs were the rage for a very short while.

In 1966 the television series "Batman" premiered to unbelievable popularity. One of the reasons for its success was the unending cast of villains every week. Which (if any) of the following actors did not play a villain on the show?

a. Julie Newmar (The Cat Woman)
b. Cesar Romero (The Joker)
c. Joan Crawford (The Cat Woman)
d. Burgess Meredith (The Penguin)
e. Eartha Kitt (The Cat Woman)
f. Frank Gorshin (The Riddler)

The answer is c.

In 1966 this famous sex-symbol actress made this remark to the press after her last divorce. "I always knew Frank would end up in bed with a boy." Name the actress and the "boy." Who was "Frank"?

Ava Gardner was not thrilled to hear of her ex-husband's new marriage. His name was Frank Sinatra, and the "boy" was the young and short-haired Mia Farrow.

Elizabeth Taylor, Richard Burton, Sandy Dennis, and George Segal were all nominated for Oscars for *Who's Afraid of Virginia Woolf?* Who, if any, took home the gold statue?

Miss Taylor and Miss Dennis

Two British sisters were up for the Best Actress Award in 1966. Name these two talented ladies and their films of that year.

Vanessa Redgrave for *Morgan!* and Lynn Redgrave for *Georgy Girl.*

A new ruling allowed millions of Americans to change their diet in 1966. What was this ruling?

U.S. Roman Catholic bishops declared that American Catholics no longer had to abstain from eating meat on Fridays, except for the seven Fridays of the Lenten season.

The new Metropolitan Opera House opened in the fall of 1966 with a specially commissioned opera by an American composer that was written for the particular voice of a great American soprano. Name the opera, the composer, and the singer.

Antony and Cleopatra was composed by Samuel Barber for Leontyne Price. Although the opera was a considerable musical success, the sets were so heavy that they broke the central stage turntable, which took months to repair.

What was the social event of the year in Washington, D.C.?

The White House marriage of Luci Johnson to Patrick J. Nugent. A second White House wedding would follow in

1967 with the marriage of Lynda Bird Johnson to Charles Robb.

There was a 1966 rumor about the Beatles that had teenage fans in a panic. What was all the fuss about?

Word was going around at the speed of an old 78-RPM record that if the Beatles' song "Revolution 9" was played backward, it relayed a secret message that Paul McCartney was dead. The fact that Paul was barefoot on the cover of *Abbey Road*, the album in which the dread song appeared, was taken as an additional clue. Paul was not amused.

A former marine recorded the number one hit of 1966. Name him and his stirring song.

Sergeant Barry Sadler sang "The Ballad of the Green Berets," the backlash anthem of those who despised the Vietnam war protestors. Ironically, Sadler served time in prison for homicide in the 1970s.

Name the 1966 Academy Award–winning song from a movie set in Africa.

"Born Free"

The Boston Celtics lost the 1966 NBA play-offs to the Philadelphia 76ers. How long had it been since they lost the championship?

They had lost to St. Louis way back in 1958.

The legendary Boston Red Sox outfielder Ted Williams was elected to the Hall of Fame in his first year of eligibility in 1966. Of the following players, which one was not chosen in his first year of eligibility during the 1960s?

a. Jackie Robinson
b. Bob Feller

c. Roy Campanella
d. Stan Musial

Roy Campanella was not voted in until his sixth year of eligibility, largely because of his abbreviated career. Robinson and Feller both got in on their first chance in 1962, Musial on his in 1969.

The International Swimming Hall of Fame was inaugurated in 1965. Name three movie stars who were selected for it in the first two years.

Johnny Weissmuller, the most famous of all Tarzans, and Buster Crabbe, who also played Tarzan but perhaps is best remembered as Flash Gordon, were both elected in the first year. Esther Williams was elected in 1966. Both Weissmuller and Crabbe had been Olympic Gold Medalists.

This left-hander is the only pitcher in baseball history to retire with a Cy Young Award for his final season. Name him.

Sandy Koufax of the Los Angeles Dodgers was an ordinary pitcher from 1954 through 1960. But with a change in his pitching motion, he became the best pitcher in baseball over the next six years, putting together an astonishing 129–43 record from 1961 to 1966. Despite the fact that he was in pain from an arthritic condition from 1964 on, Koufax managed to strike out a record 382 batters in 1965. He won the Cy Young Award in 1963, 1965, and 1966, and was MVP as well in 1963. He pitched a then record four no-hitters, the final one in 1965 being a perfect game. But he was told that if he kept pitching, he might lose total use of his arthritic left pitching arm, and had the good sense to retire in glory. He was elected to the Hall of Fame in 1972.

This wholesome family of thirty-seven sang their hearts out on TV from 1966 to 1969. They made the Lennon

Sisters look like riffraff from the wrong side of the tracks. Name this family.

The King Family

The "Last of the Red-Hot Mamas" died in 1966. Name her.

Sophie Tucker. She made quite a reputation for herself by telling risqué jokes on stages all across the world. In her later years, she found God and toned down her act.

This brave woman was the first to establish a birth control clinic in America. After many, many years of strife, she died in 1966. Name her.

Margaret Higgins Sanger

Name the very American charitable organization that celebrated the one hundredth anniversary of its founding in 1966.

The Salvation Army

What newly minted literary term did Truman Capote apply to his huge best-seller *In Cold Blood*?

He called it a "nonfiction novel," which caused critics who liked the term and critics who hated it to go for one another's throats. Capote was much amused.

A female author, whom Truman Capote would later be sued for calling a "truck driver in drag" on Johnny Carson, had her first huge success in 1966. Who was she, and what was her best-selling novel called?

Jacqueline Susann hit it big with the then very racy novel *The Valley of the Dolls.*

Playwright Peter Shaffer wrote a farce that premiered at England's Chichester Festival Theater with a cast including Albert Finney, Maggie Smith, and Lynn Redgrave. It had the cast stumbling around in virtual total darkness for ten hilarious minutes toward the end of the play. What was it called?

Black Comedy

Why were thoroughbred racing fans annoyed with a horse named Amberoid in 1966?

First, by winning the Belmont Stakes, Amberoid spoiled Kauai King's attempt to become the first Triple Crown winner in nearly twenty years; second, he was such a long shot that very few people put a bet on him, creating double the distress.

The American League Batting Champion, the American League MVP, and the World Series MVP were all the same man in 1966. Name him.

Frank Robinson of the Baltimore Orioles.

1967

"Sergeant Pepper's Lonely Hearts Club Band." Israel and its Arab neighbors fight the Six-Day War, which Israel wins decisively. Hanoi is bombed by the United States as the Vietnam War drags on, and China gets the H-bomb. Queen Elizabeth and Prince Philip visit Canada for its centennial, which is marked by the opening of Expo 67, while Charles de Gaulle stirs up separatist passions in Quebec.

Tom Stoppard turns Shakespeare's *Hamlet* inside out in *Rosencrantz and Guildenstern Are Dead*, and Ira Levin scares everyone to death with *Rosemary's Baby*. *Bonnie and Clyde*, *Accident*, and *Blow-Up* are among the year's many dark-hued films, and Hollywood mourns the deaths of movie legends Vivien Leigh, Paul Muni, Claude Rains, and Nelson Eddy.

John Newcombe of Australia reigns at the top of men's tennis with wins at Wimbledon and in the U.S. Open. Mickey Mantle hits his five hundredth home run, and the surprising Boston Red Sox lose a tense and exciting World Series to the St. Louis Cardinals 4–3.

Name the civil rights lawyer who was instrumental in persuading the Supreme Court to ban school segregation in 1954, and whom Lyndon Johnson appointed an associate justice of that court in 1967.

Thurgood Marshall, the court's first black justice.

Who crowned himself emperor and his wife empress in 1967?

The Shah of Iran

One of America's foremost publishers died in 1967. Name him and the three vastly influential magazines he founded.

Henry R. Luce had founded *Time*, *Life*, and *Fortune*.

Albert H. de Salvo was sentenced to life imprisonment in Massachusetts for the murder of thirteen women. By what name was he called in the press?

"The Boston Strangler"

Name the Boston Red Sox outfielder who was hit in the head by a pitched ball and was out for the last weeks of the season and the World Series.

Tony Conigliaro, who might have had a great career—he was a constant home run threat—was never the same afterward. But his injury did lead directly to mandatory use of batting helmets.

Rookies of the Year in baseball often fail to develop into superstars, and some have been gone after only a few seasons. But the 1967 Rookies of the Year both went on to become certain Hall of Fame players. One was a National League pitcher, the other an American League outfielder. Name them.

Tom Seaver and Rod Carew

Damascus was the all-time money winner in thoroughbred racing for a single year in 1967, with a total of $817,941, and no horse would top that until the legendary Secretariat in 1973. How many of the Triple Crown races did Damascus win?

Both the Preakness and the Belmont Stakes. He got caught in traffic in the Kentucky Derby and just missed becoming the first Triple Crown horse since 1948, and race fans had to wait for Secretariat.

This football team won its third NFL Championship and then went on to win the first play-off against the AFL 35–10. Name the team, its coach, and its quarterback.

The Green Bay Packers were coached by the legendary Vince Lombardi. Quarterback Bart Starr won the MVP award in the play-off against the Kansas City Chiefs of the AFL. The play-off game was not called the Super Bowl until after the merger of the two leagues in 1971, but the first games were retroactively numbered as Super Bowls I, II, III, and IV.

This recording by the Best Vocal Group of 1967 was awarded Best Record of the Year. This was a very "up" group. Name them and the record.

The Fifth Dimension for "Up and Away."

This composer, who wrote the scores for *A Guide for the Married Man* and *Valley of the Dolls* in 1967, went on to more exalted projects and several Academy Awards. Name him.

John Williams

The highest-rated television program of the 1960s was broadcast on August 29, 1967. Nearly twenty-six million households tuned in to this final installment of a popular series. What was the name of the series, and who did it star?

"The Fugitive" starred David Janssen. The final episode, in which the identity of the one-armed man was revealed, was still ranked seventeenth on the list of all-time Nielsen champions as of 1990.

This talented lady won the Emmy three years in a row for her work on "Mission Impossible." Name her and the character she played.

Barbara Bain played Cinnamon.

Barbra Streisand was teamed with an unusual costar for her 1967 television special, "The Belle of Fourteenth Street." Can you name him?

Jason Robards, in his musical comedy debut.

Director Mike Nichols saw this young actor in a British farce, *Eh?*, and pulled strings to have this virtual unknown as the lead in his next movie. Name him and the movie.

Dustin Hoffman, making his film debut in *The Graduate*

Can you name the Academy Award–winning song of 1967, which involved a lot of dubious conversations?

"Talk to the Animals" from *Doctor Dolittle*.

In 1967 Dame Edith Evans was up for Best Actress in *The Whisperers*. She lost to Katharine Hepburn in *Guess Who's Coming To Dinner*. However, she did present the Best Film Editing Award that evening. As this distinguished actress walked onstage, she was greeted with a blaring song from the orchestra. Can you remember it?

"There Is Nothing Like a Dame," from *South Pacific*. Never let it be said that Hollywood has no class.

This woman, who did not write her own autobiography but was extremely well known for her peculiar brownie

recipe, died in Paris in 1967. Name her and the author of her autobiography.

Alice B. Toklas, whose autobiography was written by her lifelong companion Gertrude Stein. Her recipe for hashish brownies in *The Alice B. Toklas Cookbook* were all the rage among recreational drug users, with marijuana usually substituted for the hashish.

Who did more than 135,000 people crowd Central Park in New York City to hear sing in the summer of 1967?

Barbra Streisand

This movie about Depression-era criminals garnered five Oscar nominations for acting. Name the movie, the five nominees, and the one winner.

Bonnie and Clyde, which managed to be violent, funny, and touching, brought a Best Actor nomination to Warren Beatty, a Best Actress nomination to Faye Dunaway, Best Supporting Actor nominations to both Gene Hackman and Michael J. Pollard, and a Best Supporting Actress nomination to Estelle Parsons, who was the only winner among the five, for her hilarious portrait of a woman not cut out for a life of crime.

LizaMinnellimadeherfilmdebutatage2 p6.6^{61}½inher mother's arms in the motion picture *In the Good Old Summertime*. But what was her first feature picture as a grown-up?

Charley Bubbles, with Albert Finney in *her* arms, in 1967.

In 1967 a very famous crooner made a hit record with his daughter. Name them and the song.

Frank Sinatra and Nancy Sinatra. The song was "Something Stupid." Strangely enough, it was Sinatra's first gold single.

What major American product was phased out on television commercials in the late sixties?

Cigarettes. By 1971 the ads were banned completely by the FCC.

"The Dick Van Dyke Show" won the Emmy Award for best comedy series four years in a row. What new show starring a bunch of raucous young men dethroned Dick and Co. in 1967?

"The Monkees"

This twenty-three-year-old woman won the singles, doubles, and mixed doubles titles at both the U.S. Open and Wimbledon tennis chamionships in 1967. Name her.

Billie Jean King proved herself that year to be the best all-around woman tennis player in history. In the course of her career she won six singles and ten doubles titles at Wimbledon. More than anyone else, she was responsible for turning women's professional tennis into a big money tour.

Why were U.S. authorities thoroughly delighted with the shooting deaths of two men, one in Arlington, Virginia, the other in the hills of Bolivia?

One was George Rockwell, head of the American Nazi party, and the other was Che Guevara, who was busy fomenting revolution in South America.

Why was a best-selling novel by William Styron the subject of much racial controversy?

The novel was about the pre–Civil War rebellion of the slave Nat Turner. Many leading blacks felt that this was a subject that belonged to black writers, and were particularly incensed by Styron's title, *The Confessions of Nat Turner*.

A minor English writer named Vyvyan Holland died at the age of seventy-nine in 1967. His father, however, had been, and continues to be, one of the most famous of all English writers. He was also infamous, to a degree that led to Vyvyan changing his name to Holland. Who was his father?

Oscar Wilde

Perhaps the most respected actor in Hollywood, known as both a star and as an actor's actor, passed away just after completing his final movie. Name him.

Spencer Tracy

Her comedy variety show premiered in 1967 and ran for eleven years. She said that she couldn't believe that people would put up with her that long. Name this beloved comedienne.

Carol Burnett

The star of this 1967 television show weighed in at 650 pounds. But none of his coworkers seemed to mind, because he was so lovable. Name the show.

"Gentle Ben." He was, of course, a bear.

English composer William Walton premiered a one-act comic opera based on a play by Gogol. What was it called?

The Bear

Who was greeted with enormous fanfare, and why, when he returned to England after an absence of just over seven months?

The returnee was Francis Chichester, completing his 226-day

solo voyage around the world in his yacht *Gypsy Moth*. The intrepid sailor was knighted for his efforts.

This great left fielder was not only the American League MVP in 1967, but also became the last man in either league to win the batting Triple Crown, leading the league in average, home runs, and runs batted in. Name him.

"Yaz," the slugging Carl Yastrzemski, who also played Fenway Park's left-field wall, "the Green Monster," like an artist. Yaz led the surprising Boston Red Sox to the American League pennant on the final day of the season against the Minnesota Twins. He also had to hit a home run that day, because Harmon Killebrew of the Twins hit two, putting him one ahead of Yaz, which would have cost the Boston star his Triple Crown. He got the home run.

1968

"Stoned Soul Picnic." The *Pueblo*, a U.S. Navy intelligence ship, is captured by North Korea, the Soviet Union invades Czechoslovakia to stop its liberalization under Alexander Dubcek, and students riot in Paris. Martin Luther King is assassinated in Memphis by James Earl Ray, and Robert F. Kennedy is shot to death in Los Angeles by Sirhan Sirhan just after winning the California primary.

Matt Crowley induces considerable culture shock with *The Boys in the Band*, and John Updike even raises a few eyebrows with *Couples*, while *Airport* is the champion best-seller among fiction titles. Neil Simon's *Plaza Suite* and Howard Sackler's *The Great White Hope* are huge theatrical successes, but the world is nowhere near ready for Joe Orton's *Loot*. Movie audiences like the pairing of Faye Dunaway and Steve McQueen in *The Thomas Crown Affair*, but are even more taken with Jack Lemmon and Walter Matthau in *The Odd Couple*.

At the Mexico City Summer Olympics, the United States garners forty-five gold medals to the Soviet Union's twenty-nine in the rarified air. St. Louis is back in the World Series but is defeated 4–3 by the Detroit Tigers.

What was the slogan of the thousands of young people who turned out to assist the campaign of anti-Vietnam presidential candidate Senator Eugene McCarthy?

"Stay clean for Gene."

At the outset of the year, the Republican presidential candidate who many people believed could "stop" Richard Nixon's attempt to get the Republican nomination for a

second time was the handsome, popular Michigan governor, George Romney. What was the major verbal gaffe Romney made that derailed his campaign?

He said he had been "brainwashed" into supporting the Vietnam War, and immediately lost all credibility as a potential president.

Name the practitioner of "new journalism" whose collection of flamboyantly written essays became a 1968 best-seller.

Tom Wolfe had a great success with *The Electric Kool-Aid Acid Test.*

A woman's name comprised the title of a hugely popular song by Paul Simon and Art Garfunkel composed for an offbeat hit movie. Name the song and the movie.

"Mrs. Robinson," from *The Graduate.*

What invisible celestial objects did radio astronomers discover in 1968?

Pulsars, which are believed to be rotating neutron stars that give out radio waves at precise intervals.

***Apollo* 7 and *Apollo 8* spacecraft were launched in 1968. Did either of them attempt to go to the moon?**

Yes, *Apollo 8* went into orbit around the moon before returning to a Pacific Ocean splashdown.

A great American lady died in 1968. Her early life had been the subject of a play and a movie that had earned the young actress playing her a Best Supporting Actress award for 1962. Name her.

Helen Keller, who was played by Patty Duke. Anne Bancroft, who played her teacher, Annie Sullivan, won both the Tony Award and the Oscar for Best Actress in the role.

A famous American actress who once described herself as "pure as the driven slush" also died in 1968. Name her.

The delightfully naughty Tallulah Bankhead, who also said, "If I had to live my life again, I'd make all the same mistakes—only sooner."

Name the only American to win a Gold Medal at the 1968 Winter Olympics in Grenoble, France.

Peggy Fleming, whose technical control and ethereal grace had already brought her three World Figure Skating titles and five U.S. Championships. When the entire U.S. skating team was killed in an air crash on the way to the World Championships in 1961, many thought it would be a decade before there would be another American World Champion in figure skating, but Peggy Fleming came along and reestablished the American dominance that Tenley Albright and Carol Heiss had exemplified in the 1950s.

"This is the richest nation in the world, and we'd be even richer if it weren't for the poor people." Who said that?

Pat Paulsen on "The Smothers' Brothers Comedy Hour" in the late sixties. He ran a tongue-in-cheek campaign for president of the United States. He also got many write-in votes.

"If you've seen one city slum, you've seen them all." Who said this to the press?

Vice-presidential candidate Spiro T. Agnew

On Easter week in 1968, *Time* magazine had a cover story that shocked and disgusted many Americans to the point that they canceled their subscriptions. What was all this fuss about?

The cover read "Is God Dead?"

On the night of March 31, 1968, President Lyndon B. Johnson made a televised speech from the White House that ended with an announcement so startling that many people wondered if it was an April Fool's joke. What was the announcement?

"I shall not seek, and will not accept, the nomination of my party for another term as your president."

Name the top male movie star and major American playwright who were delegates from Connecticut for Senator Eugene McCarthy at the Democratic Convention in Chicago.

Paul Newman and Arthur Miller

Which of the following men was punched and wrestled to the floor at the Democratic Convention by a security guard?

a. Yippie Abbie Hoffman
b. Author Norman Mailer
c. CBS reporter Dan Rather

Dan Rather was just one more who took it on the chin at the chaotic convention.

In 1968 the Beatles flew to India, not to give a concert but to learn something. What did these young men want to learn?

The teachings of the Maharishi Mahesh Yogi. Meditation quickly became the "in" thing to do.

At what 1968 public event did this unlikely combination of celebrities appear for a common cause? The group included Connie Francis, Lawrence Welk, Pat Boone, John Wayne, and Art Linkletter.

The Republican Convention, to support Richard Nixon

This actress/singer exploded at Lady Bird Johnson over the Vietnam War during a luncheon at the White House. Who was this woman?

Eartha Kitt. President Johnson saw to it that she was blackballed by American nightclubs, and for the next several years she had to make her living abroad.

This movie baffled many critics but wowed the under-thirty set, many of whom went to see it stoned. Name it.

Stanley Kubrick's *2001: A Space Odyssey*. Some critics who found it incomprehensible at first wrote a second review, once it had been explained to them, and upgraded their opinions—an almost unheard-of occurrence.

This versatile young singer/composer of Hispanic background won both the Best Male Vocal and Best New Artist Grammys with a pulsating hit. Name the artist and his song.

Jose Feliciano had a huge success with "Light My Fire," although the Grammy for Song of the Year went to Bobby Russell's more conventional "Little Green Apples."

Toward the end of the presidential campaign, Democratic nominee Vice President Hubert Humphrey started to separate himself from President Johnson on the subject

of Vietnam and rose rapidly in the polls. In the popular vote, how far ahead of Humphrey did Nixon finish?

a. 732,104 votes
b. 510,314 votes
c. 118,550 votes

The answer is b. Answer c was the margin of Kennedy's win over Nixon in 1960.

Two weeks before the 1968 presidential election, a new shock come to the Kennedy family. What was it?

The wedding of Jacqueline Kennedy to Aristotle Onassis

This 1968 hit single recording upset many a PTA meeting. Name the song and the singer. Why was there such an uproar?

"The Harper Valley PTA," as sung by Jeannie C. Riley. Miss Riley sang of the hyprocrisy of life in a small town when the subject of sex came up.

In 1968, how much did a gallon of gas cost?

a. Forty-eight cents
b. Fifty-three cents
c. Thirty-seven cents

The answer is thirty-seven cents.

Which, if any, of these campaign button slogans is phony?

a. Johnson for Ex-President!
b. Vietnam. Love It or Leave It.
c. You Can't Lick Our Dick (Richard Nixon).
d. Nixon Plus *Spiro* Equals *Zero*.
e. Send John Wayne To Vietnam.
f. Prostitutes! Vote for Nixon *Or* Kennedy. We Don't Care Who Gets In!

g. Let's Win in Vietnam, Australia, Hawaii, and California!

None of the above.

During his presidency, Lyndon B. Johnson did something to outrage the ASPCA. What did he do?

He picked up his beagles by the ears, much to the delight and disgust of the photographers.

In 1968 a young man made a recording, singing in a falsetto voice and accompanying himself on a ukulele. It was a major hit and brought him to national acclaim. Name him and the song.

Tiny Tim for his never-to-be-forgotten rendition of "Tiptoe Through the Tulips"

In the late sixties, poetry made a big comeback on college campuses with a great deal of help from a young blond poet. Name him.

Rod McKuen

What popular underground commodity cost twenty dollars an ounce in 1968?

Marijuana

In 1968 the Beatles started their own record label. What did they call it?

Apple

Rowan and Martin's television show, "Laugh-In," was a major success from 1968 to 1973. Can you name the very talented comedy ensemble who kept so many in stitches?

Jo Anne Worley, Arte Johnson, Goldie Hawn, Ruth Buzzi,

Chelsea Brown, Judy ("Sock it to me") Carne, and Alan Suess.

The beautiful Ingrid Bergman's eyes bulged when she opened the envelope announcing the Best Actress award at the Academy Awards ceremony for 1968. Why?

It was a tie between Katharine Hepburn for *The Lion In Winter* and Barbra Streisand for her film debut in *Funny Girl*. Miss Bergman's eyes had another reason to bulge on that evening. As she followed Miss Streisand offstage, she noticed that Barbra's evening pants were very see-through. Very.

In 1968 some street vendors were arrested for selling a particular issue of *Rolling Stone* magazine. Why?

On the cover were nude photographs of John Lennon and Yoko Ono.

This 1968 Heisman trophy winner from Southern California could run like the wind, whether on a football field or, later, through airports. Name him.

O. J. (Orenthal James) Simpson went on to spend eleven spectacular years playing pro football, with the Buffalo Bills from 1969 to 1977, and with the San Francisco 49ers from 1978 to 1979. He would lead the AFL in rushing four times, and his 2,003 yards for 1973 remains the AFL record. His record twenty-three touchdowns for the 1975 season was tops in both leagues until John Riggins of the Washington Redskins managed one more in 1984.

In 1968 both Jack Nicklaus and Arnold Palmer lost major play-offs. Name the two golfers who topped Nicklaus in the Open and Palmer in the PGA Championship.

Lee Trevino took the Open, Julius Boros the PGA.

A skinny young man with glasses and a murderous serve scored a tennis first. What was it?

Arthur Ashe became the first black male to win both the U.S. Open and Wimbledon titles.

At the Grenoble, France, Winter Olympics, a daring Frenchman won three Gold Medals and set female hearts fluttering on several continents. Name the athlete and the events for which he won his medals.

Handsome Jean-Claude Killy dashed and slashed his way to victory in all three Alpine Skiing events, the Downhill, the Giant Slalom, and the Slalom.

Every four years starting in 1956, this American athlete won an Olympic Gold Medal by throwing something farther than he had the time before. What was he throwing, and what was his name?

Throwing the discus, Al Oerter made Olympic history by winning his sport at four successive Olympics, increasing his distance from 184 feet 10 ½ inches in 1956 to 212 feet 6 ½ inches in 1968.

American Bob Beamon won the Gold Medal in the Long Jump at Mexico City in 1968. Why do many feel that his record of 29 feet 2 ⅓ inches will never be surpassed?

Because the thin air of high-altitude Mexico City aided the long jumpers in setting records even as it presented a problem to distance runners and those in other endurance sports.

Americans Tommie Smith and John Carlos took the Gold and Bronze Medals in the Two-Hundred-Meter Dash

at the Mexico City Olympics. What did they do on the winner's platform as "The Star-Spangled Banner" was being played that outraged many Americans?

They raised their fists in a black power salute to protest racism in America.

Don Drysdale passed Carl Hubbel's National League record and then Walter Johnson's major league record in 1968 in what pitching category?

The record for scoreless innings. Drysdale ended up with a new record of 58 ½ innings.

This Detroit Tigers pitcher won more games in 1968 than anyone since Dizzy Dean in 1934. Who was the pitcher, and how many games did he win?

Denny McLain won thirty-one games, one more than Dizzy had.

What did a woman in a polka-dotted dress have to do with the assassination of Robert F. Kennedy?

Such a woman was reported to have been seen with Sirhan Sirhan earlier in the evening by several witnesses, but the investigators were never convinced that such a woman even existed, giving conspiracy enthusiasts another mystery to worry about.

The gun that Sirhan Sirhan used to shoot Robert Kennedy had originally been purchased in 1965 but had changed hands several times since then. What had been the original reason for buying it?

It had been bought by a middle-class white man frightened by the riots in the Watts section of Los Angeles, in order to protect his family. When things calmed down, he sold it to a coworker, and it eventually ended up in the hands of Sirhan.

What was the nickname for members of the Youth International party, led by Jerry Rubin, who were victims of the police riot at the Democratic National Convention in Chicago?

Yippies

This 1968 movie shocked and outraged many Christians with its explicit scene of the young Mia Farrow being raped by the devil. Name the film.

Rosemary's Baby, written by Ira Levin. It was one of the biggest hits of the year.

"The Doris Day Show" debuted in 1968 with much fanfare. It ran for four years. She was as adorable as ever, but there was a little trouble with the continuity from season to season. In fact, this problem made people laugh. Why?

In the first season, Doris was a widow with two children. By the fourth season, the kids were gone, with no explanation whatsoever. None.

This black singer/actress landed her own television series in 1968. It was in no way the "Beulah" mode. She played a widowed nurse with (what else?) two children. Name her and the show.

Diahann Carroll in "Julia."

Two grandes dames of American fiction died in 1968, one famous for her historical romances of the American scene, the other a specialist in soap operas about fallen women with pure souls. Name the two ladies.

Edna Ferber, author of *Show Boat* and *Saratoga Trunk*, and Fannie Hurst, whose *Madame X* and *Back Street* were made and remade as Hollywood movies so many times, it's hard to keep track.

T*he Man in the Glass Booth*, a much-honored play about the trial of Adolf Eichmann for Nazi war crimes, was written by a stage and screen actor who had first come to the attention of the mass public as the wire-jawed villian in *From Russia with Love*. Name the author/actor.

Robert Shaw, an actor who could play anything and a very fine writer, also was nominated for an Academy Award for Best Supporting Actor as Henry VIII in 1966's *A Man for All Seasons*.

What sporting trophy did the United States manage to wrest back from the Australians for the first time in five years?

The Davis Cup—Australia had pretty much dominated the world of men's tennis during the 1960s.

One of the greatest and most controversial of college football coaches was named Coach of the Year in the coaches' poll, but the writers opted for another great coach with a very different kind of reputation. Name these coaches from Ohio State and Penn State.

Woody Hayes of Ohio and Joe Paterno of Penn.

1969

"Aquarius." Sirhan Sirhan and James Earl Ray are convicted of the murders of Robert Kennedy and Martin Luther King, Dwight D. Eisenhower dies, and Charles de Gaulle resigns the presidency of France following the failure of a constitutional referendum he had championed. Warren Burger is confirmed by the Senate as Richard Nixon's choice to be chief justice of the Supreme Court.

Philip Roth's *Portnoy's Complaint* has its hero doing obscene things to himself at the back of the bus, and Mario Puzo's *The Godfather* features a bedroom scene with the severed head of a horse. *Butch Cassidy and the Sundance Kid* is the most popular western in a long time; *They Shoot Horses, Don't They?* is not a western. Hollywood loses three of its greats with the deaths of Judy Garland, Boris Karloff, and Robert Taylor.

Rod Laver wins the Grand Slam of tennis for the second time. Majestic Prince really does look like the first Triple Crown thoroughbred horse since Citation in 1948, but is beaten in the Belmont Stakes by Arts and Letters. The absolutely "amazin' " New York Mets take the World Series 4–1 over the favored Baltimore Orioles.

What rare rocks, acquired in 1969, cost $25 million an ounce by some estimates?

Moon rocks.

The first human being to set foot on the moon was astronaut Neil Armstrong, on July 20, 1969, followed a few minutes later by fellow *Apollo 11* astronaut Edwin E.

"Buzz" Aldrin. Name the third astronaut on the mission, who remained in orbit around the moon with the command capsule.

Michael Collins

News of what accidental event that would have major political consequences broke on the afternoon of July 19, and was initially overshadowed by the imminent moon landing?

The news that Senator Edward Kennedy had driven off a bridge at Chappaquiddick Island the previous night and that Mary Jo Kopechne had been drowned in the accident.

Name the writer who liked to strand his characters in a wasteland, ensconce them in tin cans, or bury them up to the neck in sand, who won the Nobel Prize for Literature in 1969.

Irish-born French-language playwright and novelist Samuel Beckett, author of *Waiting for Godot*, *Endgame*, and *Happy Days*.

Norman Mailer was awarded the Pulitzer Prize in nonfiction for the previous year's *Armies of the Night*. What was the subject of this book?

The 1967 Lincoln Memorial peace demonstration against the Vietnam War.

Playing Gudrun Brangwen, this actress won the Academy Award for Best Actress in only her fourth movie. Name the actress and the movie.

Glenda Jackson won for Ken Russell's superheated version of D. H. Lawrence's *Women in Love*.

Two legendary Hollywood ladies were competing with each other in Broadway musicals to see who could croak out the fewest flat notes. Who were they, and what were the names of their musicals?

Lauren Bacall in *Applause* and Katharine Hepburn in *Coco*. Bacall stayed more on key and would beat Hepburn for the Tony Award.

Beloved by audiences around the world, this woman turned fifty in 1969. She was still going strong in a profession that usually brought an earlier retirement. Who was she, and to whom did she give the credit for a new lease on her professional life?

Prima ballerina of the Royal Ballet Dame Margot Fonteyn credited her partnership with Rudolf Nureyev for giving her new strength and continued artistic growth. Nureyev defected from Russia during an engagement of the Kirov Ballet in Paris during 1961. Nureyev was twenty years Fonteyn's junior, but from their first appearance together, it was clear that one of the great partnerships in the history of ballet had been born. They complemented each other perfectly, and in the course of the 1960s their dancing took on a legendary aura.

A brother and sister were both nominated for 1969 Academy awards, the sister for Best Actress, the brother for Best Original Screenplay. Name them and the movies for which they were nominated.

Jane Fonda received her first nomination for *They Shoot Horses, Don't They?* and Peter Fonda was nominated with cowriters Dennis Hopper and Terry Southern for *Easy Rider*.

The hit foreign film of the year was a political thriller with an extremely short title. Name it.

Z, directed by Costa-Gravas, who was nominated for a Best Director Oscar (won by John Schlesinger for *Midnight Cow-*

boy). The film was also nominated for Best Picture, Best Adapted Screenplay, Best Film Editing, and Best Foreign Film, winning in the last two categories.

Name the Kurt Vonnegut novel dominated by nightmarish memories of the bombing of Dresden, Germany, first published in 1969.

Slaughterhouse Five

The eagerly awaited film version of *Hello Dolly*, starring Barbra Streisand, was a smash hit at the box office. True or false.

False. It was the resounding disaster of 1969, losing about $13 million.

This 1969 X-rated film was the first and only to win the Best Picture Academy Award. Name it.

Midnight Cowboy. Both Jon Voight and Dustin Hoffman were nominated for Best Actor, thus canceling each other out. The prize went to the sentimental favorite, John Wayne, for *True Grit*.

Can you name the hit song from *Midnight Cowboy*?

"Everybody's Talking," by Harry Nilsson

In 1969 a Chicago newspaper ran an article on a Nixon fund-raising speech. The headline screamed, "Can't Stand Pat, Says Nixon." What did that mean?

Nixon was warning his fellow Republicans against "the temptation to stand pat on what we have done." When he saw the headline, the president was not one bit amused. But he changed the word "pat" to "firm" in future speeches, thus spoiling its meaning.

President Nixon was given a rather strange Father's Day present by his two daughters in 1969. Newspapers across the country ran pictures of him posing with his new toy. What was it?

A custom-made blue surfboard.

Vice President Spiro Agnew's famous phrase, "nattering nabobs of negativism," was in fact thought up by a White House speech writer who is now a major conservative columnist. Name him.

William Safire, who also writes a weekly column on the vagaries of the English language for *The New York Times Magazine*.

Jerry Rubin, Abbie Hoffman, Rennie Davis, David Dellinger, Tom Hayden, Bobby Seale, Lee Weiner, and John R. Froines were called the "Chicago Eight" when they were put on trial for conspiracy and the intent to incite a riot at the Democratic Convention the previous year. A few weeks later they had become the "Chicago Seven." Why?

Black Panther Bobby Seale was so disruptive that Judge Julius J. Hoffman first had him gagged and bound and handcuffed to a chair and then sentenced him to four years for contempt, removing him from the trial and sending him to prison. The entire trial was a circus from start to finish.

In 1969 a rock concert was held at Woodstock, New York. It got worldwide coverage. How many people attended this event, and what was the running joke about coverage?

Four hundred thousand attended the concert. The joke was

that many decided it was quite natural to walk around in their birthday suits. A good time was had by all.

Which of the following entertainers was paid the most money to appear at Woodstock?

a. The Jimi Hendrix Experience
b. Janis Joplin
c. Joan Baez

Jimi Hendrix got $18,000, Joan Baez got $10,000, and Janis Joplin got $7,500.

What were found one morning in August 1969 at 10050 Cielo Drive, above Benedict Canyon, in Los Angeles?
The mutilated bodies of actress Sharon Tate and four friends, murdered by the followers of Charles Manson at his behest. Sharon Tate's husband, director Roman Polanski, was out of the country.

The week of January 12, 1969, an athlete whose father had been a coal miner made a prediction that was initially regarded as a vainglorious boast. But it subsequently came true. What was the prediction, and who made it?
New York Jets quarterback Joe Namath predicted that the Jets would beat the heavily favored Baltimore Colts in Super Bowl III. But with the help of fellow Hall of Famers Coach Weeb Ewbank and receiver Don Maynard, the Jets did just that, 16–7. Namath was named MVP, and the upstart American Football League began to be taken seriously, leading to a merger of the two leagues in 1971.

In 1969 a rookie manager who was to have one of the most controversial managerial careers in baseball guided the Minnesota Twins to the top of the American League West. Name him.
Billy ("sock it to you") Martin

The NBA Rookie of the Year would end his career twenty years later with twenty-three pro basketball records in his high pockets. Give the name under which he won Rookie of the Year honors.

Milwaukee Bucks center Lew Alcindor, who had not yet changed his name to Kareem Abdul-Jabbar.

Who replaced William Eckert as commissioner of baseball in 1969?

Wall Street lawyer Bowie Kuhn; Eckert, a former general, had served only three years.

The 1969 New York Mets were amazingly good instead of amazingly bad. Led by pitchers Tom Seaver, Jerry Koosman, Nolan Ryan, and Gary Gentry, and the hitting of Tommy Agee, Cleon Jones, and Dave Clendenon, picked up in midsummer, plus the ever-steady Jerry Grote behind the plate and Bud Harrelson at shortstop, the Mets swept all before them. Name the fine hitter but lightly regarded defensive player who saved game three of the World Series with a diving catch in right field.

When the chips were down, with the bases loaded, the supposed weak link in the outfield made one of the most spectacular catches in World Series history, and Ron Swoboda entered the Mets pantheon of heroes forever.

Peggy Lee won the Grammy Award for Best Vocal Performance in 1969. What was the name of the song?

"Is That All There Is?"

What royal ceremony, performed once in a generation, took place in England in 1969?

Prince Charles was formally installed as Prince of Wales.

The new prime minister of Israel had been born in Russia and raised in the United States. Who was this person?

Golda Meir became the fourth prime minister of Israel.

An Asian leader whose name had been used during the 1960s as part of an international student chant died. Who was he?

North Vietnamese President Ho Chi Minh, whose name was used and abused in chants that began "Ho Ho Ho Chi Minh . . ."

Off the coast of New Hampshire, a man named Alphonse Belevich made the record books by catching something that weighed ninety-eight pounds twelve ounces. What was it?

An Atlantic cod; it is one of the oldest still-standing records for fishermen.

The National League won the All Star Game 9–3. How many wins in a row did that make it for the National League?

a. Four
b. Seven
c. Nine

The answer is b. They would go on to win every contest until 1983, except for 1971.

Who was the World Series MVP in the Mets' remarkable win over the Baltimore Orioles?

a. Tom Seaver
b. Jerry Grote
c. Donn Clendenon
d. Tommy Agee

The answer is c. The addition of the aging first baseman to the Mets roster had proved one of those moves that smack of genius in hindsight.

This weekly music show was corn right off the cob, but viewers ate it with a pitchfork. The cohosts were Buck Owens and Ray Clark. Name the show.

"Hee Haw"

The ladies got a weekly rush with this sexy British singer's show from 1969 to 1971. "It's not unusual . . ." the singer sang, but what with panties flying out of the audience, it did seem a little peculiar. Name the singer.

Tom Jones